THE BLENDER BOOK

By the same author

Steaming!
Microwave Cooking Properly Explained
The Microwave Planner
Microwave Recipes For One
The Combination Microwave Cook
The Barbecue Cook

Uniform with this book

THE BLENDER BOOK

Annette Yates

RIGHT WAY

Typeset in 10/11pt Swiss 721 by Letterpart Ltd., Reigate, Surrey. Printed and bound in Great Britain by Cox & Wyman Ltd., Reading, Berkshire.

The *Right Way* series is published by Elliot Right Way Books, Brighton Road, Lower Kingswood, Tadworth, Surrey, KT20 6TD, U.K. For information about our company and the other books we publish, visit our web site at www.right-way.co.uk

CONTENTS

INTRODUCTION

Fashion statement or practical tool? In my kitchen a blender happens to be both.

Though the blender has been around for well over half a century, it has often taken a back seat to the more glamorous food processor. However, it is a mistake to think that one can replace the other. There are indeed some tasks that the two appliances do equally well, but a blender can create a smoothness that no food processor can match. Today, with health high on everyone's schedule, the blender really comes into its own for whizzing up your favourite smoothies and fruit drinks, vegetable and fruit purées, dips, dressings, sauces and soups. And unlike a food processor, a blender copes well with small quantities, so it's particularly good at preparing baby food.

It has been a joy developing and testing the recipes in this book. They are not designed to use a blender simply for the sake of it. Instead, each recipe (in my opinion anyway) benefits from the use of a blender to achieve a specific result, to save time or to make laborious jobs effortless and difficult jobs easy. In other words, I aim to get the best out of my blender.

Choose one that's sleek, stylish, utilitarian, state-of-the-art, retro – there's one to suit you and a designer colour to match every kitchen. Leave your blender out on the worktop for all to see and it will always be on standby, ready to whizz into action, producing dishes for every day and every occasion at the touch of a button.

So get blending, be healthy and have fun!

Annette Yates

P.S.
I am indebted to KitchenAid Europa for the loan of their Ultra Power Plus Blender for the recipe testing for this book. For stockists of KitchenAid Europa blenders, please telephone 0845 4500099.

Huge thanks also go to Jenny Webb, my colleague and friend, for her expert advice; as well as to Annie Willis and Ted French for their excellent illustrations.

1

ABOUT BLENDERS

Blenders (sometimes referred to as liquidisers) are available as self-contained, free-standing units or as an attachment to a table-top food mixer or multi-purpose kitchen machine. The former will have its own power base with motor, while the latter will use the motor of the food mixer or kitchen machine. Short, sharp, stainless steel blades rotate at high speed, cutting through the food that is in contact with them and forcing the mixture up the sides of the jar and then down the centre (like a whirlpool action), back on to the blades in surges.

What they are capable of doing depends mainly on the power of the motor. The more powerful models (350 watts and over) will handle most tasks, including chopping, mixing, puréeing, liquefying and, often, crushing ice and grinding coffee. Some blenders are sold with their own accessory blade or attachment for ice crushing or coffee grinding.

Because blender jars are tall and narrow and because the blades are small and rotate so fast, air cannot be incorporated into the food. So a blender will not 'whip' or 'whisk' foods such as egg whites or cream. However, when it comes to making purées, sauces, soups and drinks, a blender is the best tool for the job.

WHAT TO LOOK FOR

▯▯ Look for a sturdy, heavy base with non-slip feet – to keep the blender from wobbling or 'walking' across the worktop when operating at high speeds or handling heavy jobs such as crushing ice.

- On top of the base sits a heat (and cold) resistant jar made of toughened glass, heavy plastic or stainless steel. Glass jars are sturdy though they can be quite heavy and can break or crack if dropped. Plastic jars are lighter and very tough but they can get scratched or discoloured. The main advantage of both glass and plastic is that the contents of the jar are visible. Stainless steel is probably the most durable – it copes with very hot food and keeps frozen drinks icy cold, but you cannot see what's going on inside it without removing the lid.

- The size and shape of jar varies from model to model. Look for a wide opening for easy filling, easy-to-read measurement markings on the side of the jar and a shape that is easy to scrape out. A handle and large spout make for ease of use and pouring.

- Make sure the lid fits tightly in the top of the jar.

- Most models include a small twist-lock plug in the centre of the lid that can be removed to release steam or to add ingredients while the machine is running (and without splattering the kitchen). These plugs often double as small measuring cups.

- Make sure the blades can be removed for easy cleaning, with a rubber gasket to provide a tight seal that prevents liquids from leaking out from the jar on to the base.

- If you want to be able to blend very small quantities (such as one or two egg yolks for mayonnaise), look for blades that are set low in the jar.

- Controls may be push-button, dial or touch-control pads. Each type is easy to use though touch pads are the easiest to clean.

- For best results, choose a blender with at least two speeds.

- A pulse button allows greater control and helps to prevent over blending.

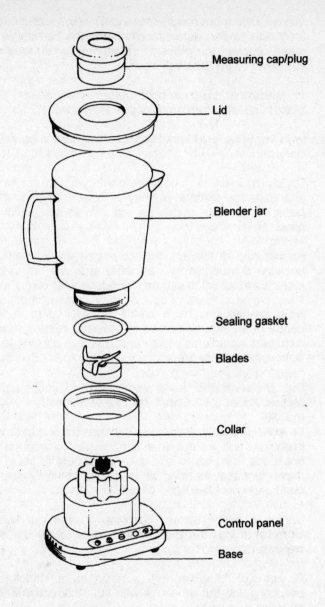

- Measuring cap/plug
- Lid
- Blender jar
- Sealing gasket
- Blades
- Collar
- Control panel
- Base

Fig. 1. A typical blender.

- Some of the more advanced models come with a 'step start' feature that automatically starts the blender at a lower speed to prevent splattering then quickly increases to the selected speed.

- An 'electronic mixing sensor' automatically adjusts the blender speed when more power is needed.

- Indicator lights are helpful to show whether the power is on or off.

- Check the instruction book before buying, to see what quantities the blender is likely to cope with and what tasks it is capable of dealing with. It's always useful to have some recipes too.

- Having said all this, choose the largest you can afford because blenders work best when they are not much more than half full. If you enjoy making your own soup, it can be time consuming and fiddly to blend it in very small quantities.

TIPS FOR GOOD RESULTS:

- Cut, break or tear large items of food into smaller pieces. About 2.5-3.5cm/1-1½ inches is ideal.

- To work efficiently, there must be enough food to cover the blades and, except when chopping small amounts of dry foods, it's best to add a small amount of liquid to make sure that the food at the top becomes incorporated and gets blended.

- Unless a recipe states otherwise, always put liquid ingredients into the blender first followed by the dry ingredients.

- Do not overfill the blender – a maximum of half full is a general guide but do check with your instruction book to make sure.

- Fit the lid securely on to the jar before turning on the blender.

- The speed you choose will depend on the type of food that is to be blended. If in doubt, start on a low speed and, if little happens, increase the speed. Whenever possible, be guided by your manufacturer's instruction book.

- When blending hot foods or liquids, such as soups and sauces, remove the cap in the lid and place a thick cloth over the top. This allows the steam to escape instead of forcing the lid up and causing the hot contents to spill out. Always start blending on a low speed and gradually increase it. At the risk of stating the obvious, please do not place your bare hand over the blender lid.

- To add extra ingredients while the machine is running, use low-to-medium speed, remove the cap and feed items or drizzle in liquid through the hole.

- Avoid over-processing foods. A blender works incredibly fast (so don't be tempted to walk away from it while the motor is running). Stop and check the consistency every few seconds, scraping down the sides of the jar if necessary.

- Use a rubber spatula to scrape down the sides and to remove food from the blender jar.

- Always switch off the blades and make sure the motor is completely stopped before lifting the blender jar off its base.

- Always make sure the blender is switched off before inserting any utensil into the blender. Never put a utensil (or your fingers!) anywhere near the blades while the blender jar is still sitting on its base.

- Clean your blender jar quickly and easily by adding warm water (up to half full) and a drop of washing up liquid and blending on low speed until the sides are clean. Rinse and dry.

- For complete cleaning, dismantle and wash and dry pieces separately.

▯ Always switch off and unplug the blender before dismantling it.

▯ The manufacturer's instruction book will indicate which parts of the blender are dishwasher proof.

▯ The power base (containing the motor) should never be immersed in water.

▯ Finally (and it's another obvious point, I know) do not store food in your blender for any length of time. Empty, wash and dry it after each use.

2

GETTING THE BEST OUT OF YOUR BLENDER

Your blender will quickly and easily undertake all those difficult and/or time-consuming jobs that would otherwise require a great deal of effort. Keep your blender on the kitchen worktop ready to:

▌ **Chop vegetables and fruit**, raw or cooked. Put small whole pieces or chopped large pieces into the blender, cover and pulse on low speed until the desired consistency is achieved. Small amounts work best.

▌ **Purée cooked or canned vegetables**. Use medium-high speed, adding a little water or vegetable stock and scraping down the sides if necessary.

▌ **Purée raw soft fruit**. Blend fruit such as strawberries, raspberries or currants on medium-high speed, scraping down the sides if necessary. The resulting 'sauce' can be sweetened with sugar to taste.

▌ **Purée canned or cooked fruit**. Drain the fruit, reserving the juice. Blend on medium-high speed, adding sufficient juice to make a smooth purée (scrape down the sides occasionally if necessary).

▌ **Chop, shred or purée cooked meat**. Cut the meat into small cubes and put into the blender (with a little stock, water or milk if wished). Starting on low speed, pulse until the mixture is as coarse or smooth as you wish, adding extra liquid and scraping down the sides if necessary.

✂ **Purée cottage or ricotta cheese**. When making dips, spreads, fillings for pasta or cheesecake mixtures, spoon the cheese into the blender (with or without added ingredients) and blend at medium speed, scraping down the sides and adding a little milk (or liquid from the recipe) if necessary.

✂ **Chop hard cheese**. Cut the cold cheese (such as Parmesan or Cheddar) into cubes, put into the blender and pulse on high speed until very finely chopped. Suitable for up to about 85g/3 oz cheese. Use it as you would use grated cheese.

✂ **Chop or grind nuts**. Put the nuts into the blender and pulse on medium-low speed until coarsely or finely chopped or finely ground. It's best to blend nuts in small batches – in a large batch, the nuts at the bottom may have ground to a fine powder before the top ones are chopped.

✂ **Break up seeds**, the ones that are difficult to digest whole (such as linseed and sesame), for adding raw to muesli and other breakfast cereals. Add sufficient to cover the blades of the blender and pulse on high speed until the seeds are broken.

✂ **Chop herbs** for sauces, casseroles, salads and pesto (recipe on page 52). Put the washed and dried herbs into the blender and pulse on medium-low speed, scraping down the sides if necessary, until finely chopped.

✂ **Chop fresh coconut**. Remove the coconut from its shell and cut into cubes. Put into the blender and pulse on medium speed until it reaches the consistency you want.

✂ **Chop chocolate**. Break the chocolate into the blender and pulse on medium-low until chopped to the required coarseness.

✂ **Make breadcrumbs** for stuffings, bread sauce or breadcrumb coatings. Cut or tear bread into small pieces, put into the blender and pulse on medium-high speed until the crumbs are as coarse or fine as you wish.

Make biscuit crumbs for cheesecake bases or dessert toppings. Break large biscuits into pieces, put into the blender and pulse on low speed until the crumbs are as coarse or fine as you need.

Make cake crumbs for desserts. Break the cake into pieces, put into the blender and pulse on low speed until the crumbs are formed.

Grind coffee beans. Put a small amount into the blender and pulse on high speed until it is ground as fine as you want.

Prepare baby food. Blend fruit, vegetables, meat, fish or a mixture of foods from the adults' meal, starting on a low speed, until smooth. If necessary, scrape down the sides of the blender and add a little water or milk to make the mixture as thick as you wish.

Mix liquids. When a recipe calls for liquid ingredients to be whisked or mixed together, pop them into the blender on high speed. This is particularly useful when honey, golden syrup, treacle, marmalade or jam needs to be blended into liquid.

Purée soups. Allow the cooked soup to cool slightly before pouring into the blender (you may need to do this in batches). Starting on a low speed, blend until smooth. Take care not to overfill the blender and never start on a high speed as hot liquid may spill out and cause scalds.

Make quick sandwich spreads, with hard-boiled eggs, cheese, canned beans or left-over pieces of cooked meat or fish. Just whizz them up in the blender with a little soft butter, ricotta or cream cheese. See also Chapter 5 for more ideas.

Mix bastes and marinades. For example, try the recipes in Chapter 4.

Make salad dressings. The blender is excellent at emulsifying salad dressings so that they are less likely to separate on standing. Put your favourite proportions of oil, vinegar, sugar, mustard, seasoning and herbs into the blender and blend on high speed until smooth and thickened. Some delicious recipes appear in Chapter 6.

Mix sauces. When making a white sauce, put the milk, flour and seasonings into the blender and blend on low speed until smooth. Transfer the mixture and cook in the usual way.

Mix batter for pancakes and Yorkshire pudding. See pages 85 and 86.

Remove lumps from gravies and sauces. If you end up with a lumpy sauce, simply tip it into the blender and, starting on low speed, blend until smooth. Reheat, stirring, and bring it to the boil.

Reconstitute frozen fruit juice. Tip the frozen block of fruit concentrate into the blender and add some or all (depending on the capacity of your blender) of the measured water. Blend on medium speed until completely combined.

Pulp fruit for a healthy juice drink. Put washed and chopped raw fruit of your choice (oranges, lemons, grapefruit, pears, pineapple, melon) into the blender and, starting on a low speed, pulse until coarsely chopped. Increase the speed and blend until finely chopped, scraping down the sides if necessary. Press the mixture through a sieve to extract the juice.

Make milk shakes, smoothies and other drinks. See Chapter 10.

Crush ice (in some blenders only). Many blenders are capable of crushing ice – check in your instruction book for directions on how to do it. Small ice cubes work best and some models require the addition of a small amount of water.

Make vanilla sugar. Put some caster sugar into the blender with a chopped vanilla pod. Blend on high speed until the pod is very finely chopped and dispersed through the sugar. Sieve to remove any large pieces of pod and store the vanilla sugar in an airtight container.

3

NOTES ABOUT THE RECIPES

All the recipes in this book were tested in a free-standing blender with two functions and five speeds, electronic mixing sensor, 1.25 litre jar and touch-pad controls.

Servings
Generally, servings are for two or four, though the number will depend largely on the type of recipe. I have tried to keep to sensible, manageable quantities though these too will depend on the capacity of your blender.

Ingredients
For convenience, the ingredients are listed in the order in which they are used. Though they are given in imperial as well as metric, you will find the metric measurements easier to use.

Spoon measurements
These are always level unless otherwise stated.

Eggs
These are usually medium, unless otherwise stated. One or two recipes may contain raw or partly cooked eggs – please remember that it is advisable to avoid eating these if you are pregnant, elderly, very young or sick.

Recipe methods
When giving instructions for blending, to save repetition, I have assumed that the ingredients have been put into the blender and the lid has been fitted securely. In other words, the blender is never used without its lid in position.

Whenever possible I have indicated the speed of blending (from low to high). You may need to vary this slightly according to your blender.

When a recipe benefits, I have used a pulsing action. If your blender does not have a pulse button, you will need to switch the motor on and off in short bursts.

When blending hot liquids (such as soups and sauces), care is needed. Do not overfill the blender – half full is about right. To prevent the liquid from spurting out beneath the lid, remove the cap in the lid and place a thick cloth over the top. Start blending on a low speed and then gradually increase it. To avoid being splashed by the hot liquid, never be tempted to hold your bare hand over the blender lid.

Microwaves
When appropriate, I have slotted in the occasional microwave instructions. I used an 800W microwave. If your microwave has a lower wattage, you will need to cook for a little longer. If it has a higher wattage, then simply lower the power level slightly and cook for the time given in the recipe.

4

BASTES, PASTES AND MARINADES

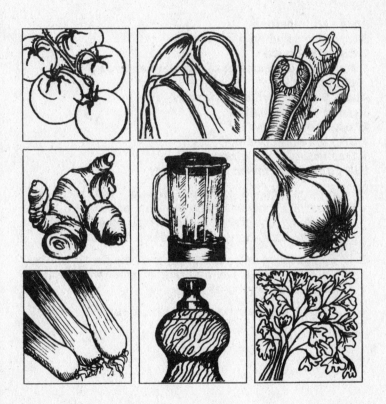

Eastern Tomato Baste

Make this quick and tasty sauce out of store-cupboard ingredients. The tamarind imparts a slightly sour flavour – if you leave it out, the result will be slightly different but still delicious. Brush the cooked sauce over chops, spare ribs, sausages or chicken pieces before and during grilling or barbecuing.

Serves 4

200g can tomatoes
3 tbsp rice or white wine vinegar
2 tbsp fish sauce
3 sun-dried tomatoes in oil, drained and roughly
  chopped
About 6 spring onions, chopped
1 garlic clove, crushed
2 tbsp brown sugar
1 tbsp tamarind paste
1 tbsp grated fresh ginger
Salt and freshly milled black pepper

1. Put the canned tomatoes, vinegar, fish sauce and 100ml/3½ fl oz water into the blender, followed by the remaining ingredients. Blend on high speed until almost smooth, scraping down the sides if necessary.

2. Tip the sauce into a saucepan and heat gently, bringing just to the boil. Cover and simmer very gently for 10-15 minutes, stirring occasionally.

3. Adjust the seasoning to taste before serving.

Mild Curry Paste

This is ideal for chicken and/or vegetables. First, brown about 350g/12 oz bite-size chicken in a little oil, then add the Mild Curry Paste, some vegetables (such as 250g/9 oz diced sweet potato or a drained 400g can of chickpeas), seasoning and a small amount of stock or water. Cover and simmer gently for 30-40 minutes before adjusting the seasoning and adding a handful of chopped fresh coriander.

Take care when handling the chilli – wash your hands thoroughly afterwards or, better still, wear thin rubber gloves to prepare it.

Serves 4

1 large onion, chopped
2 garlic cloves, crushed
1 green chilli, seeds removed, and chopped
2 tbsp tomato purée
1 tbsp mild curry paste
1 tbsp mango chutney
1 tbsp grated root ginger
1 tsp brown sugar
1 tsp salt

1. Put all the ingredients into the blender and pulse on high speed to make a thick paste, scraping down the sides occasionally.

2. Cover and chill until required.

Indonesian Curry Paste

Fry the paste in a little oil for a few minutes before adding 450-675g/1-1½ lb cubed meat, a chopped tomato or two and 250ml/8 fl oz coconut milk. Simmer gently, on the hob, or in the oven at 180°C/350°F/Gas 4, for about 1½ hours or until the meat is tender. Serve with fragrant rice.

Take care when handling chillies – wash your hands thoroughly afterwards or, better still, wear thin rubber gloves to prepare them.

Serves 4

1 large onion, chopped
Finely grated rind of ½ lemon
Juice of 1 lemon
2 garlic cloves
1 tbsp grated fresh ginger root
4 red chillies, seeds removed if wished
2.5cm/1 inch cinnamon stick
2 tbsp desiccated coconut, toasted
2-3 curry leaves (fresh or dried)
1 tsp ground almonds
1 tsp ground coriander
1 tsp ground cumin
½ tsp ground turmeric
½ tsp salt
About 2 tbsp oil

1. Put the onion into the blender with the lemon rind and juice and garlic. Pulse on high speed until finely chopped, scraping down the sides if necessary.

2. Gradually add the remaining ingredients, loosening the mixture with a little oil, to make a smooth paste.

Vindaloo Curry Paste

A very hot curry mixture that originates from Goa. Marinate 450-675g/1-1½ lb cubed meat (pork is particularly good) in the paste for several hours or (chilled) overnight. Fry a sliced onion in oil or ghee, add the meat and its marinade and one or two bay leaves. Simmer gently, on the hob, or in the oven at 180°C/350°F/Gas 4, for 1-1½ hours or until the meat is tender. Serve with freshly cooked basmati rice.

Serves 4-6

1 tsp coriander seeds
1 tsp cumin seeds
1 tsp fenugreek seeds
1 tsp chilli powder
About 6 black peppercorns
½ tsp cardamom seeds
1 cinnamon stick
3 whole cloves
1 tsp grated root ginger
150ml/¼ pt malt or wine vinegar
1 plump garlic clove, crushed
1 tsp ground turmeric
½ tsp salt

1. Put the first nine ingredients into a pan and cook over a medium heat for about 5 minutes, stirring frequently, until the spices are toasted.

2. Put the vinegar into the blender and add the toasted spice mixture and the remaining ingredients.

3. Pulse on high speed, scraping down the sides occasionally and adding a little water if necessary to make a thick pouring consistency.

Green Chilli Paste

Marinate chicken pieces (thighs are good) in this fragrant mixture for a couple of hours before cooking. Lift them out of the marinade, brown them in a little oil, then add the marinade and cook gently, adding some chicken stock and coconut milk. Serve with rice or noodles.

Take care when handling chillies – wash your hands thoroughly afterwards or, better still, wear thin rubber gloves to prepare them.

Serves 4

3 tbsp groundnut, peanut or olive oil
1 tbsp fish sauce
Finely grated rind and juice of 2 limes
3-4 green chillies, seeds removed, and chopped
1 tbsp grated root ginger
2 tsp ground cumin
2 tsp ground coriander
6 spring onions, chopped
5 lime leaves, torn (optional)
Handful of fresh coriander leaves
1 garlic clove, crushed
Salt and freshly milled black pepper

1. Put the oil into the blender followed by the remaining ingredients in the order in which they are listed.

2. Pulse on medium speed until very finely chopped and a smooth paste is formed.

3. Chill until required.

Spiced Green Pepper and Mint Paste

I mix this paste with lean minced lamb before shaping it into burgers or meatballs and frying, grilling or barbecuing. Serve them in split pitta bread with a dollop of Greek yogurt flavoured with chopped fresh mint.

Enough for 450-550g/1-1¼ lb minced lamb

3 tbsp olive oil
1 small green pepper, seeds removed, and chopped
4 spring onions, chopped
2 garlic cloves
2 tsp ground cumin
Salt and freshly milled black pepper
Small handful of fresh mint leaves

1. Put the ingredients into the blender in the order in which they are listed.

2. Blend to a smooth paste, scraping down the sides occasionally.

3. Chill until required.

Apricot, Soy and Ginger Baste

I love this on pork or lamb chops. Marinate them in the mixture first, then baste the meat with it during grilling or barbecuing.

420g can apricot halves in natural juice
3 tbsp light soy sauce
2 tsp grated ginger root

1. Tip the apricots and their juice into the blender and add the soy sauce and ginger.

2. Blend on medium speed until smooth, scraping down the sides if necessary.

Tandoori Marinade

The finished flavour that this marinade gives to the food makes the long list of ingredients worth it. Use it to coat skinned chicken portions – cover and leave to marinate for 2 hours or longer (chilled) – before grilling, barbecuing or oven cooking.

Sufficient for 8 chicken pieces

1 medium onion, roughly chopped
3 plump garlic cloves
2.5cm/1 inch piece fresh root ginger, roughly chopped
4 tbsp lemon juice
225g/8 oz natural yogurt
4 tbsp sunflower oil
1 tbsp ground turmeric
1 tbsp ground coriander
1 tsp ground cumin
½ tsp ground cinnamon
½ tsp grated nutmeg
½ tsp freshly milled black pepper
¼ tsp ground cloves
¼ tsp chilli powder

1. Put the onion, garlic and ginger into the blender and pulse until finely chopped, scraping down the sides occasionally.

2. Add the remaining ingredients and blend until smooth.

Rosemary, Garlic and Orange Marinade

Particularly good rubbed over beef steaks or pork (skin removed) before grilling or barbecuing.

About 6 tbsp olive oil
6 garlic cloves
4 tbsp fresh rosemary leaves
Zest of 1 orange, thinly removed with a potato peeler
1 tsp salt
½ tsp freshly milled black pepper

1. Put the oil into the blender followed by the remaining ingredients.

2. Pulse on medium speed until fairly smooth, scraping down the sides if necessary, and adding a little extra oil if necessary.

Pineapple and Coconut Marinade

Chicken and pork are good candidates for marinating in this mixture. Use it to baste (brush over food) during grilling or barbecuing too.

200ml carton coconut cream
½ lime
¼ fresh pineapple, peeled and chopped
1 tsp sweet chilli sauce

1. Put the coconut cream into the blender.

2. Scrape the flesh out of the lime and add to the blender, followed by the remaining ingredients.

3. Pulse on medium speed until smooth, scraping down the sides if necessary.

Hot Mango Marinade

This is lovely on chicken breasts – leave the skin on and make several cuts into the meat before adding the marinade, covering and leaving to stand for 1-2 hours.

Take care when handling the chilli – wash your hands thoroughly afterwards or, better still, wear thin rubber gloves to prepare it.

4 tbsp hot mango chutney
Finely grated rind and juice of 1 lime
4 tbsp natural yogurt
2 tbsp fresh coriander leaves
1 small green chilli, seeds removed, and chopped

1. Put all the ingredients into the blender and pulse on medium speed until smooth, scraping down the sides if necessary.

Three Herb and Onion Marinade

Try this one on fish such as salmon, monkfish, swordfish or tuna. Leave it to marinate for up to 2 hours before cooking.

3 tbsp olive oil
Juice of 1 lemon
1 mild onion, chopped
Small handful each of parsley, coriander leaves and dill fronds

1. Put the oil and lemon juice into the blender followed by the onion and herbs.

2. Pulse on medium speed until fairly smooth, scraping down the sides occasionally if necessary.

SPREADS, PÂTÉS AND DIPS

Spiced Cheese Spread

This recipe is based on Liptauer, a soft cheese made from sheep's milk that is popular in Hungary and other European countries. Don't be put off by the colour – it's absolutely delicious. Spread it on crisp biscuits or bread or serve it as a dip.

Serves 6-8

225g/8 oz cream cheese
115g/4 oz soft butter
1 tbsp capers, rinsed
1 tsp sweet paprika
1 tsp wholegrain mustard
1 tsp caraway seeds
1 tbsp chopped chives
½ tsp salt
½ tsp freshly milled black pepper

1. Put the cheese into the blender and add the remaining ingredients. Blend on medium speed until smooth, scraping down the sides occasionally.

2. Chill or freeze until required.

Smoked Haddock Pâté

Serve with crusty bread or hot toast.

Serves 4-6

115g/4 oz unsalted butter
450g/1 lb smoked haddock fillets
200g carton cream cheese
Freshly milled black pepper
1 tbsp lemon juice

1.   Melt half the butter in a frying pan, add the haddock, cover and cook gently for about 5 minutes or until the fish just flakes.

2.   Remove the skin and any bones before tipping the fish and all its juices into the blender.

3.   Add the cheese, pepper and lemon juice and blend until smooth, scraping down the sides if necessary.

4.   Spoon the mixture into a serving dish.

5.   Melt the remaining butter and pour evenly over the top of the pâté.

6.   Cover and chill for at least 2 hours before serving.

Chicken Liver Pâté

A smooth pâté that's traditionally served with hot buttered toast, though I like it too with melba toast or toasted pitta bread.

Serves 6

55g/2 oz butter plus extra for melting
1 medium onion, finely chopped
1 garlic clove, crushed
450g/1 lb chicken livers, trimmed
Pinch of mixed spice
Salt and freshly milled black pepper
4 tbsp chicken stock
142ml carton soured cream
2 medium eggs
2 tbsp dry sherry
2 tbsp brandy
2 level tsp cornflour

1. Heat 55g/2 oz butter in a pan, add the onion and garlic and cook for about 5 minutes, stirring occasionally until soft but not brown.

2. Add the chicken livers, spice and seasoning to the pan and cook for about 10 minutes, stirring occasionally, until the livers are just cooked.

3. Pour the chicken stock into the blender and add the liver mixture and all its juices. Blend on medium speed until smooth, scraping down the sides if necessary.

4. Add the cream and eggs and blend until well mixed.

5. Stir the sherry and brandy into the cornflour to make a smooth paste and, with the machine running, add to the liver mixture.

6. Pour the mixture into a 1.1 litre/2 pt ovenproof dish and cover. Place the dish in a large dish or tin with boiling water to reach half way up the dish.

7. Cook in a preheated oven at 160°C/325°F/Gas 3 for 1-1½ hours until firm.

8. Keep covered and allow to cool completely.

9. Melt some extra butter and pour it over the surface of the pâté, making sure it is completely covered.

10. Chill until required.

Spiced Mango Mayonnaise

This is a versatile recipe. It's delicious spread in chicken sandwiches, tossed with a salad of diced chicken and chopped celery or served as an accompaniment to spoon alongside cooked meats.

Serves 4

6 tbsp mayonnaise (to make your own, see page 51)
6 tbsp natural yogurt
4 tbsp mango chutney
2 tbsp curry paste
2 tbsp fresh coriander leaves

1. Put all the ingredients in the blender and blend on high speed until smooth, scraping down the sides if necessary and adding a little water to thin the mixture to the desired consistency.

2. Chill until required.

Smoked Mackerel Pâté

No cooking involved here – just whizz up the ingredients in the blender. Serve it as a snack or starter with crusty bread or plain biscuits.

Serves 4-6

200g carton Greek yogurt
½ tsp finely grated lemon rind
225g/8 oz smoked mackerel fillets
1-2 tsp horseradish sauce
1 tbsp lemon juice, or to taste
Salt and freshly milled black pepper

1. Put the yogurt and lemon rind into the blender.

2. Roughly flake the fish, discarding the skin, and add to the blender.

3. Blend on medium speed until almost smooth, scraping down the sides occasionally and adding horseradish sauce, lemon juice and seasoning to taste.

4. Spoon into a dish, cover and chill until required.

Petits Pois and Mint Dip

Good served with sticks of cucumber and other vegetables.

Serves 4

150g/5½ oz frozen petits pois
200g carton Greek yogurt
1 tsp ready-made mint sauce
Salt and freshly milled black pepper

1. Cook the peas following packet instructions, drain and cool.

2. Put the yogurt and mint sauce into the blender and add the peas. Blend on high speed until smooth, scraping down the sides occasionally and seasoning to taste.

3. Chill until required.

Roasted Pepper Dip

Serve this with thin toasted slices of Italian style bread such as ciabatta.

Serves 4-6

1 bread slice, weighing about 50g/1¾ oz
1 garlic clove, crushed
160g jar roasted peppers
5 tbsp olive oil
Salt and freshly milled black pepper

1. Break the bread into the blender and blend on high speed to make fine crumbs.

2. Add the garlic, peppers (including their juices) and oil. Blend on high speed until smooth, scraping down the sides occasionally and seasoning to taste.

3. Chill until required.

Green Olive Paste

Serves 4-6

About 4 tbsp extra virgin olive oil
About 40 pitted green olives
1 tsp capers, rinsed
1 tbsp ground almonds
1 plump garlic clove, crushed
Freshly milled black pepper

1. Put the oil into the blender, followed by the remaining ingredients.

2. Pulse on medium speed until finely chopped and as smooth as you like, scraping down the sides occasionally and adding a little extra oil if necessary.

3. Chill until required.

Tapenade (Black Olive Paste)

Serves 6-8

150ml/¼ pt extra virgin olive oil
1 tsp lemon juice
1 tbsp brandy (optional)
400g can pitted black olives
2-3 anchovy fillets
1 garlic clove
2 tbsp capers, drained
Freshly milled black pepper

1. Put the oil, lemon juice and brandy (if using) into the blender.

2. Add the olives, anchovies, garlic, capers and pepper.

3. Pulse on medium-high speed until finely chopped and as smooth as you like, scraping down the sides occasionally.

4. Chill until required.

Spicy Avocado Dip

I like to serve this with small crisp salad leaves and garlic bread.

Take care when handling the chilli – wash your hands thoroughly afterwards or, better still, wear thin rubber gloves to prepare it.

Serves 4-6

1 ripe avocado, halved, stone removed, and peeled
1 small green chilli, seeds removed, and chopped
Juice of ½ lemon
4 tbsp single cream
1 tsp Worcestershire sauce
Dash of sweet pepper sauce
Salt and freshly milled black pepper

1. Put all the ingredients into the blender and blend on high speed until smooth, scraping down the sides if necessary.

2. Adjust seasoning to taste before serving.

Artichoke Dip

Serves 6-8

285g jar artichokes in oil
300ml/½ pt thick natural yogurt
2 tbsp chopped chives
Salt and freshly milled black pepper

1. Drain the artichokes, reserving the oil.

2. Put the yogurt into the blender followed by the remaining ingredients plus 1 tbsp of the reserved oil. Blend on medium speed until smooth, scraping down the sides occasionally and adding a little extra oil if necessary.

3. Adjust seasoning to taste and chill until required.

Turkish Aubergine Dip

My version of the Turkish dish called Baba Ghanoush. Serve it with warm pitta bread.

Serves 4-6

2 medium aubergines
2 tbsp thick Greek yogurt
1 tbsp olive oil, plus extra for drizzling
1 tbsp lemon juice or to taste
1 garlic clove, crushed
2-3 sprigs fresh parsley
Salt and freshly milled black pepper
Black olives, to garnish

1. Prick the aubergines with a fork, place on a baking sheet and bake at 200°C/400°F/Gas 6 for 30-40 minutes until soft. Put the hot aubergines into a plastic bag for 10-15 minutes then, while still warm, split and scoop out the flesh.

2. Put the yogurt, oil and lemon juice into the blender, followed by the garlic, aubergine flesh, parsley and seasoning. Blend on high speed until smooth, scraping down the sides if necessary.

3. Adjust the seasoning to taste, transfer to a serving bowl and chill until required.

4. To serve, drizzle the top with extra olive oil and garnish with a few black olives.

Hummus

Here is a light, quick-to-make version of this classic Middle Eastern dip. It's best prepared several hours in advance or even the day before serving – to allow the flavour to develop. Serve it as a starter with crusty bread or pitta bread, as part of a selection of dishes (mezze) or spread in sandwiches with salad ingredients.

Serves 6

410g can chickpeas
1 garlic clove, crushed
2 tbsp tahini (sesame paste)
3-4 tbsp Greek yogurt
3 tbsp lemon juice
½ tsp ground cumin
1 tbsp olive oil, plus extra for drizzling
Salt and freshly milled black pepper
Paprika, to garnish

1. Drain the chickpeas, reserving the liquid.

2. Put the chickpeas into the blender and add the remaining ingredients, except for the paprika. Blend on high speed until fairly smooth, scraping down the sides occasionally and adding about 2 tbsp of the reserved liquid to make a thick consistency.

3. Adjust the seasoning to taste and chill until required.

4. To serve, drizzle extra olive oil over the surface of the hummus and sprinkle with a little paprika.

Chickpea and Red Pepper Dip

If time allows, prepare the dip several hours in advance of (or the day before) serving, to allow the flavour to develop.

Serves 4-6

1 tsp olive oil
1 large red pepper, seeds removed, and chopped
400g can chickpeas, drained
1 large garlic clove, finely chopped
2 tsp sesame oil
1 tbsp lemon juice
3-4 tbsp mayonnaise
Salt and freshly milled black pepper

1. Heat the oil in a pan, add the red pepper and cook for about 10 minutes, stirring occasionally, until very soft and golden brown.

2. Add the chickpeas and garlic and cook gently for about 5 minutes, stirring occasionally.

3. Tip the mixture into the blender and add the sesame oil, lemon juice and mayonnaise. Blend on high speed until smooth, scraping down the sides if necessary.

4. Season to taste, cover and chill until ready to serve.

Fresh Herb Dip

A fresh-flavoured dip to serve with vegetable crudités, crisps or crackers.

Serves 6-8

284ml carton soured cream
200g carton cream cheese
3 spring onions, chopped
Small handful of fresh herb leaves such as basil,
  coriander or parsley
Salt and freshly milled pepper
Milk

1. Put the cream into the blender followed by the cheese, onion, herbs and seasoning. Blend on medium-to-high speed until smooth, scraping down the sides occasionally and thinning with a little milk to make a soft consistency.

2. Adjust the seasoning to taste, cover and chill until required.

Soured Cream Fruit Dip

Simply indulgent! Here is a sweet dip to serve with crisp pieces of fresh fruit such as apple, pear or peach; chunks of banana on cocktail sticks; or whole strawberries and grapes.

Serves 4

3-4 tbsp apricot preserve
284ml carton soured cream
¼ tsp ground cinnamon
Red and green grapes, to decorate

1. Put the apricot preserve, cream and cinnamon into the blender and blend until really smooth.

2. Spoon the mixture into a bowl, cover and chill until required.

3. Decorate with grapes before serving.

Tomato Salsa

Make the salsa several hours before serving to allow the flavours to develop. Serve it with a mountain of tortilla chips.

Take care when handling chillies – wash your hands thoroughly afterwards or, better still, wear thin rubber gloves to prepare them.

Serves 6-8

400g can tomatoes
1 small red onion, chopped
2 red chillies, chopped
About 4 tbsp fresh coriander leaves
1 tsp sugar
¼ tsp chilli powder
Salt and freshly milled black pepper

1. Put the first six ingredients into the blender and pulse until well chopped but slightly chunky.
2. Transfer to a bowl and season to taste.
3. Cover and chill until required.

Guacamole

Serve with sticks of vegetables for dipping or spread it thickly on bread or crackers.

Serves 4-6

1 tomato
2 ripe avocados, halved, stones removed, and peeled
2 tbsp lemon juice
½ small red onion, chopped
½ tsp paprika

1. Put the tomato into a small bowl, cover with boiling water and leave to stand for a few minutes, after which the skin should slip off easily. Remove the skin and quarter the tomato.
2. Put the tomato into the blender with the remaining ingredients. Blend on high speed until almost smooth, scraping down the sides if necessary.

6

DRESSINGS AND SAVOURY SAUCES

A Light Vinaigrette

This recipe is a classic French dressing that has been lightened (and therefore reduced in fat) with the addition of apple juice. With normal whisking or shaking up the ingredients in a jar, the dressing would separate, but the blender emulsifies it so that it holds together well. Use it on any salad combination or to dress hot new potatoes.

Makes about 225ml/8 fl oz

100ml/3½ fl oz olive oil
100ml/3½ fl oz apple juice
2 tbsp wine vinegar
2 tsp Dijon or wholegrain mustard
2 tsp sugar
Salt and freshly milled black pepper

1. Put the first five ingredients into the blender and blend on high speed until smooth and slightly thickened.

2. Season to taste, then chill until required.

Black Olive Vinaigrette

Delicious served on a large bowl of cooked and cooled green beans and halved cherry tomatoes.

Serves 8

About 175ml/6 fl oz extra virgin olive oil
200g can pitted black olives in brine
2 shallots, chopped roughly
2 tbsp fresh lemon juice
1 tbsp Dijon mustard
1 tbsp anchovy paste (or 3-4 anchovy fillets, drained)
2 tsp finely grated lemon rind
1 tsp fresh thyme leaves

1. Put the oil into the blender followed by the remaining ingredients.

2. Blend on high speed until smooth, adding a little extra oil if necessary.

Watercress and Orange Dressing

I like to serve this on a salad of sliced tomatoes and fresh orange segments.

Makes about 250ml/9 fl oz

150ml/¼ pt sunflower or light olive oil
3 tbsp orange juice
2 tbsp wine vinegar
1 spring onion, chopped
25g/1 oz watercress leaves
½ tsp finely grated orange rind (optional)
1 tsp Dijon or wholegrain mustard
Salt and freshly milled black pepper

1. Put all the ingredients into the blender and blend on high speed until smooth.
2. Adjust the seasoning to taste, then chill until required.
3. Stir well before using.

Tomato and Fresh Herb Dressing

This is more of a light, chilled sauce that is best spooned around salad ingredients on a plate. It's particularly good with slices of ripe avocado or chunks of hot roasted vegetables.

Serves 4-6

400g can tomatoes
1 shallot, quartered
½ tsp sugar
½ tsp sweet chilli sauce (optional)
2 tbsp fresh herb leaves, such as thyme, coriander or parsley
Salt and freshly milled black pepper

1. Put the tomatoes into the blender followed by the remaining ingredients. Blend on high speed until smooth.
2. If wished, pass the sauce through a sieve to remove the solids. Adjust the seasoning to taste.
3. Cover and chill until required, stirring well before serving.

Blue Cheese Dressing

Excellent spooned on top of grilled steak. It's equally good served as a dip too.

Makes about 300ml/½ pt

150g carton natural yogurt
150g carton cottage cheese
3 tbsp mayonnaise
25-55g/1-2 oz blue cheese, such as Stilton, crumbled
Freshly milled pepper
Milk

1.   Put the first five ingredients into the blender and blend until smooth, scraping down the sides and thinning with a little milk if necessary.

2.   Cover and chill until required.

Caesar Dressing

Toss with torn romaine lettuce and freshly grated Parmesan cheese, all topped with crunchy croûtons.

Serves 6-8

About 175ml/6 fl oz olive oil
40g/1½ oz freshly grated Parmesan cheese
5 anchovy fillets, rinsed
3 tbsp fresh lemon juice
2 garlic cloves
2 tbsp Dijon mustard

1.   Put the oil into the blender followed by the remaining ingredients.

2.   Blend on high speed until smooth, adding a little extra oil if necessary.

Mayonnaise

Nothing quite beats home-made mayonnaise! This one is quite lemony. Remember to put the kettle on to boil, because you will need a tablespoon of boiling water in the final step.

Makes about 300ml/½ pt

1 medium egg
1 medium egg yolk
½ tsp ready-made English mustard or 1 tsp dry mustard powder
¼ tsp salt
2 tbsp lemon juice or wine vinegar
Freshly milled pepper
300ml/½ pt oil (I use half olive and half sunflower)

1. Put the egg and egg yolk into the blender and add the mustard, salt, half the lemon juice and a twist of pepper. Blend on medium speed until smooth.

2. Pour the oil into a jug and, with the machine running, slowly pour into the blender in a thin stream. Keep your eye on it and when it thickens add the remaining lemon juice (with the blender running all the time), then slowly add the remaining oil, followed by 1 tbsp boiling water.

3. Cover and chill until required.

Spiced Mango Mayonnaise

Make up the recipe on page 37.

Pesto

Pesto is delicious spread on small toasts or biscuits as an appetizer, or serve it tossed with hot pasta or spooned on to soups or grilled fish and meat.

Serves 4-6

1 small garlic clove, chopped
125g/4½ oz pine nuts, toasted
3 handfuls of fresh basil leaves
85g/3 oz Parmesan cheese, chopped
About 1 tbsp fresh lemon juice
About 150ml/¼ pt extra virgin olive oil, plus extra for
**   thinning**
Salt and freshly milled black pepper

1. Put the garlic, pine nuts, basil and cheese into the blender and blend (use the pulse button if you have one) until finely chopped, scraping down the sides occasionally if necessary.

2. Add the lemon juice and 150ml/¼ pt oil and blend well, scraping down the sides occasionally, until the sauce is as smooth as you like. To make a thinner sauce, add extra oil until the desired consistency is achieved.

3. Season with salt, pepper and extra lemon juice to taste.

Walnut and Parsley Pesto

Replace the pine nuts with toasted walnuts and the basil with parsley.

Aioli

The blender makes short work of making this French garlic-flavoured mayonnaise.

8 garlic cloves
2 medium egg yolks
Juice of 1 lemon
Salt and freshly milled pepper
425ml/¾ pt olive oil

1. Put the garlic, egg yolks, lemon juice and seasoning into the blender and blend on medium speed until smooth.

2. Pour the oil into a jug and, with the machine running, slowly pour into the blender in a thin stream until the mixture has thickened.

3. Cover and chill until required.

Lime and Dill Sauce

A really quick sauce that is delicious drizzled over grilled, fried, poached or baked fish.

Serves 4

Juice of 2 limes
1 tsp finely grated lime rind
1 spring onion, chopped
5 tbsp olive oil
1 tbsp chopped fresh dill
Salt and freshly milled black pepper

1. Put the lime juice, lime rind and onion into the blender and blend briefly on high speed.

2. With the machine running, gradually pour in the oil.

3. Stir in the dill and season with salt and pepper.

White Sauce

If you have trouble making white sauce without lumps, try whizzing it all up in the blender before cooking. Add flavourings (grated cheese, chopped herbs, mustard, capers, curry paste and so on) in step 3.

Makes about 300ml/½ pt

300ml/½ pt milk
15g/½ oz butter
15g/½ oz plain flour
Salt and freshly milled pepper

1. Put the ingredients in the blender in the order in which they are listed and blend on high speed until smooth.
2. Transfer the mixture to a saucepan and cook over low heat, stirring continually with a wooden spoon or whisk, until the sauce comes to the boil and thickens.
3. Adjust the seasoning before serving.

Creamy Tuna Sauce

This sauce was created originally to serve with pork – do try it, it's delicious. It's good on pasta too.

Serves 4

150ml/¼ pt chicken stock
150g can tuna, drained
2 tbsp double or soured cream
1 tbsp capers
½ tsp finely grated lemon rind
Salt and freshly milled black pepper

1. Put the chicken stock into the blender. Add the tuna, cream, half the capers and 150ml/¼ pt water.
2. Blend on high speed, adding a little more water if necessary to make a smooth sauce.
3. Tip the sauce into a saucepan and add the remaining capers, lemon rind and seasoning.
4. Bring just to the boil, stirring, and serve immediately.

Hollandaise Sauce

This sauce is lighter than hollandaise made by hand and it needs to be used straight away. Serve it with fish or vegetables.

Makes about 300ml/½ pt

3 medium egg yolks
2 tsp white wine vinegar
2 tsp fresh lemon juice
Salt and freshly milled pepper
175g/6 oz unsalted butter
1 tsp caster sugar

1. Put the egg yolks, vinegar, lemon juice and seasoning into a blender and blend on high speed for about 15 seconds until the yolks are creamy.

2. Heat the butter and sugar in a pan until melted and hot, taking care it does not brown.

3. With the blender running at high speed, gradually add the hot butter in a slow stream until the mixture is thickened, smooth and creamy.

4. Serve immediately or keep the sauce warm in a bowl over hot water.

Mediterranean Beans

Serve this just as it is in bowls with plenty of garlic bread, topped with grilled or barbecued chicken, on a bed of freshly cooked rice, or spooned into split jacket potatoes. By adding extra stock, you will have made a substantial soup.

Serves 4

1 tbsp olive oil
1 small red onion, finely chopped
1 celery stick, thinly sliced
1 small carrot, finely chopped
1 garlic clove, crushed
1 tsp sugar
300ml/½ pt passata (sieved tomatoes)
1 tsp dried herbs, such as oregano
150ml/¼ pt vegetable stock
420g can haricot beans, drained and rinsed
Finely grated rind and juice of ½ lemon
Salt and freshly milled black pepper

1. Heat the oil in a saucepan and add the onion, celery, carrot, garlic and sugar. Cook for 8-10 minutes, stirring occasionally, until very soft but not brown.

2. Stir in the remaining ingredients.

3. Bring just to the boil, cover and simmer gently for 10 minutes.

4. Tip half of the mixture into the blender and blend until smooth.

5. Return the blended beans to the pan, adjust the seasoning to taste and heat through.

Satay Sauce

A smooth sauce that's good served with chicken, pork or beef kebabs.

Serves 4-6

1 tbsp oil
1 medium onion, chopped
2 tsp brown sugar
½ tsp chilli powder
2 garlic cloves, crushed
300ml/½ pt coconut milk
1 tbsp lemon juice
175g/6 oz crunchy peanut butter
Salt and freshly milled black pepper

1. Heat the oil in a pan and add the onion and sugar. Cook gently for about 10 minutes, stirring occasionally, until the onion is very soft and beginning to turn golden brown.

2. Stir in the chilli and garlic and cook, stirring, for 1-2 minutes.

3. Pour the coconut milk into the blender and add the lemon juice, onion mixture and peanut butter. Blend on medium speed until smooth, scraping down the sides if necessary.

4. Tip the sauce into the pan (no need to wash it). Bring to the boil and simmer gently for a few minutes, seasoning to taste with salt and pepper, until the sauce reaches the desired consistency.

Tomato Sauce

This is my family's basic tomato sauce that's suitable for serving on pasta or with vegetables, fish, poultry or meat.

Serves 4-6

1 tbsp olive oil
1 small onion, chopped
1 small carrot, chopped
1 small celery stick, sliced
1 garlic clove, chopped or crushed
400g can tomatoes or 450g/1 lb fresh ripe chopped
   tomatoes
300ml/½ pt chicken or vegetable stock
1 tbsp tomato purée
1 tbsp sugar
1 tbsp chopped fresh herbs, such as thyme, basil or
   parsley
Salt and freshly milled black pepper

1.   Heat the oil in a pan, add the onion, carrot, celery and garlic and cook for about 5 minutes, stirring occasionally, until soft but not brown.

2.   Stir in the remaining ingredients. Bring to the boil, cover and simmer gently for about 15 minutes or until the vegetables are very tender.

3.   Allow to cool slightly, then tip the sauce into the blender and blend (starting on a low speed) until smooth.

4.   Return the sauce to the pan and reheat before serving.

Parsnip and Pear Purée

This recipe was developed for the microwave by my good friend Caroline Young and published in our newsletter. The purée is delicious served with grilled sausages or roast pork.

Serves 4

675g/1½ lb parsnips, sliced
25g/1 oz butter
4 dessert pears, peeled, cored and sliced
¼ tsp ground allspice
3 tbsp soured cream
Salt and freshly milled black pepper

1. Cook the parsnips in lightly salted boiling water for about 15 minutes until very soft. Drain, then tip into the blender.

2. Melt the butter in a pan, add the pears and cook gently for about 10 minutes or until very soft. Tip the pears and their juices into the blender and add the allspice and cream.

3. Blend on high speed until smooth, scraping down the sides if necessary.

4. Return the mixture to the pan, season to taste and reheat gently before serving.

Watercress Cream Sauce

A slightly peppery sauce that looks and tastes particularly good when served with vegetables such as parsnips and carrots. Try it too on freshly cooked pasta topped with some Parmesan shavings.

Serves 4

1 tbsp olive oil
2 shallots, chopped
Pinch of sugar
300ml/½ pt vegetable stock
1 bunch of watercress, leaves only
3 tbsp double cream
Salt and freshly milled black pepper

1. Heat the oil in a saucepan, add the shallots and sugar and cook gently for 5-8 minutes, stirring occasionally, until soft and only just beginning to turn golden brown.

2. Add the stock and watercress, bring just to the boil, cover and simmer gently for 5 minutes.

3. Tip the mixture into the blender and blend (starting on low speed) until smooth.

4. Return the sauce to the pan, add the cream and seasoning to taste. Bring just to the boil and simmer gently for about 1 minute until the sauce has thickened slightly.

Piri Piri Sauce

A particularly fiery sauce that should be added in small quantities to chicken, meat or fish dishes. Take care when handling chillies – wash your hands thoroughly afterwards or, better still, wear thin rubber gloves to prepare them.

Makes about 300ml (½ pt)

Juice of 4 lemons
1 red pepper, seeds removed, and sliced
8 hot red chillies, seeds removed, and sliced
2 tbsp olive oil
¼ tsp salt
1 garlic clove, crushed (optional)

1.   Put the lemon juice, pepper and chillies in a small pan, bring to the boil, cover and simmer gently for 10-15 minutes until the peppers are very soft.

2.   Tip the mixture into the blender, add the oil, salt and garlic (if using) and blend until smooth, scraping down the sides if necessary.

3.   Cool, cover and chill until required.

Red Pepper and Tomato Sauce

This recipe was developed several years ago by my daughters, Emma and Lindsay, when I was asked to create some dishes under the heading of 'Young Cooks'. Now my young nieces, Megan and Siân, like to make it too. They brown some chicken strips in oil in a frying pan, add the sauce (made to the end of step 2) and simmer gently for about 20 minutes until cooked through.

Serves 4-6

225ml/8 fl oz chicken or vegetable stock
1 small onion, chopped
1 red pepper, seeds removed, and chopped
400g can tomatoes
1 tbsp tomato purée
1 tsp sugar
Salt and freshly milled black pepper
1 tbsp olive oil

1. Put the stock, onion and red pepper into the blender and pulse until fairly smooth.

2. Add the tomatoes, tomato purée, sugar and seasoning and blend on high speed until smooth.

3. Put the oil in a saucepan and add the sauce. Bring slowly to the boil, stirring frequently, then simmer gently for 10-15 minutes.

7

SIMPLY SOUPS

Cream of Tomato Soup

Everyone's favourite soup! The sugar is an important season-ing, so don't be afraid to add extra until the soup tastes just right.

Serves 4-6

2 tbsp olive oil
1 medium onion, finely chopped
1 garlic clove, crushed
900g/2 lb ripe tomatoes or two 400g cans or a mixture
of both
2 tbsp tomato purée
1 tbsp sugar or more
600ml/1 pt chicken or vegetable stock, plus extra if
necessary
1-2 tbsp chopped fresh herbs, such as parsley, oregano,
thyme or basil
300ml/½ pt milk
142ml carton double cream
Salt and freshly milled black pepper

1. Heat the oil in a saucepan, add the onion and garlic and cook gently for about 5 minutes, stirring occasion-ally, until soft but not brown (alternatively put the ingredients into a casserole, cover and microwave on High for 3 minutes until soft).

2. Add the tomatoes, tomato purée, sugar, stock and herbs. Bring to the boil, then simmer gently for about 20 minutes (or cover and microwave on High for 15-20 minutes).

3. Leave to cool slightly, then tip the mixture into the blender. Starting on low speed, blend until smooth.

4. At this stage, I like to pass the soup through a sieve to remove seeds and any skins.

5. Return the soup to the pan, stir in the milk and cream. Season to taste with extra sugar, salt and pepper and thin with a little extra stock if necessary. Reheat (on the hob or in a casserole in the microwave) before serving.

Chilled Avocado Soup

Choose really ripe avocados for a creamy smooth and sweet soup. For a spiced version add 2-3 tsp curry paste. Serve with breadsticks, crisp savoury biscuits or toasted pitta bread.

Serves 4

2 ripe avocados
6 spring onions, chopped
1 small garlic clove, crushed
150g carton thick natural Greek style yogurt
600ml/1 pt cold vegetable stock
2 tbsp skimmed milk powder
Salt and freshly milled pepper

1. Halve the avocados, remove the stones and spoon the flesh into the blender. Add the onions (reserving a few of the green tops for garnish), garlic, yogurt, stock and milk powder.

2. Blend until smooth.

3. Season to taste with salt and pepper, then chill until required.

4. Serve garnished with the reserved onion tops.

Tomato and Basil Soup

Replacing the basil with coriander or flat-leaf parsley gives equally delicious results. If you omit the herbs altogether, you will still have made a really good tomato soup.

Serves 4-6

1 tbsp olive oil
1 medium onion, finely chopped
1 plump garlic clove, crushed
400g can chopped tomatoes
450g/1 lb ripe tomatoes, sliced (or another 400g can chopped tomatoes)
2 tbsp tomato purée
2 tbsp sugar
900ml/1½ pt chicken or vegetable stock
Salt and freshly milled black pepper
2-3 tbsp double cream or crème fraîche
Handful of fresh basil leaves

1. Heat the oil in a large pan, add the onion and garlic and cook gently, stirring occasionally, for about 5 minutes, until soft but not brown (or put into a casserole, cover and microwave on High for about 3 minutes, stirring once).

2. Stir in the canned and fresh tomatoes, tomato purée, sugar and stock.

3. Bring to the boil, cover and simmer gently for about 20 minutes (or cover and microwave on High until boiling, then on Medium for about 20 minutes).

4. Leave to cool slightly, then tip the mixture into the blender (in batches) and, starting on low speed, blend until smooth.

5. At this stage (if using fresh tomatoes) I like to pass the soup through a sieve to remove seeds and skins.

6. Return the soup to the pan and stir in the cream. Tear up the basil, stir in and reheat.

7. Season to taste with salt and pepper before serving.

Creamed Parsnip Soup with Nutmeg

This combination of parsnips, freshly grated nutmeg and cream is velvety smooth and absolutely delicious. Parsnips that are clean and free from blemishes need not be peeled; just scrub them.

Serves 4-6

1 tbsp oil
1 medium onion, chopped
1 plump garlic clove, crushed
450g/1 lb parsnips, thinly sliced
225g/8 oz main-crop potatoes, thinly sliced
1 litre/1¾ pt vegetable stock, plus extra if necessary
Salt and freshly milled pepper
Freshly grated nutmeg
Fresh lemon juice
4 tbsp double cream or crème fraîche

1. Heat the oil in a large pan, add the onion and garlic and cook gently, stirring occasionally, for about 5 minutes until soft but not brown (alternatively put the ingredients into a casserole, cover and microwave on High for about 3 minutes, stirring once).

2. Add the parsnips, potatoes and stock.

3. Bring to the boil, cover and simmer gently for about 20 minutes or until the vegetables are very soft (or cover and microwave on High until boiling, then on Medium for about 20 minutes).

4. Leave to cool slightly, then tip into the blender (you may need to do this in batches) and, starting on low speed, blend until smooth. Thin with extra stock if necessary.

5. Return the soup to the pan and season to taste with salt, pepper, nutmeg and a squeeze or two of lemon juice. Stir in the cream.

6. Reheat the soup (on the hob or in a casserole in the microwave), bringing it just to the boil before serving.

Broad Bean Soup with Mint and Lime

Make this with fresh broad beans and mint in summer or with frozen beans and dried mint during the rest of the year. Serve it with a bowl of crisp-fried pieces of bacon, pancetta or prosciutto for scattering over the top.

Serves 4-6

15g/½ oz butter
2 tsp olive oil
1 medium onion, finely chopped
1 plump garlic clove, finely chopped
450g/1 lb broad beans, fresh or frozen
1 litre/1¾ pt vegetable stock
Small handful of fresh mint leaves (or 1 tsp dried mint),
   plus shredded leaves for garnish
Half a 200ml carton crème fraîche
Finely grated rind and juice of 1 small lime
Salt and freshly milled black pepper

1.   Heat the butter and oil in a large pan, add the onion and garlic and cook gently, stirring occasionally, for about 5 minutes until soft but not brown (alternatively put the ingredients into a casserole, cover and microwave on High for about 3 minutes, stirring once).

2.   Add the beans, stock and mint.

3.   Bring to the boil, cover and simmer gently for about 20 minutes until the beans are tender (or cover and microwave on High until boiling, then on Medium for about 20 minutes).

4.   Stir in the crème fraîche, the lime rind (save a little for garnish) and the lime juice.

5.   Leave to cool slightly, then tip the mixture into the blender (in batches if necessary) and, starting on low speed, blend until smooth.

6.   Return the soup to the pan or casserole and reheat.

7.   Serve in bowls, garnished with shredded mint leaves.

Courgette and Mint Soup with Pancetta

This light, summery soup tastes best when made with a good-quality chicken stock. To make a vegetarian version, omit the pancetta, replace the chicken stock with vegetable stock and serve the soup topped with flakes of cheese.

Serves 4-6

1 tbsp olive oil
About 70g/2½ oz pancetta, cut into tiny cubes
1 small onion, chopped
1 small main-crop potato (about 140g/5 oz), peeled and
   thinly sliced
1 plump garlic clove, chopped
675g/1½ lb courgettes, sliced
1 litre/1¾ pt chicken stock
2 tbsp chopped fresh mint, plus extra leaves to garnish
Salt and freshly milled black pepper
Fresh lemon juice

1. Heat the oil in a large pan, add the pancetta and cook, stirring occasionally, until crisp. Lift out with a slotted spoon and reserve.

2. Add the onion, potato and garlic to the pan and cook for about 5 minutes, stirring occasionally, until soft but not brown.

3. Add the courgettes and cook, stirring occasionally, for 5 minutes.

4. Add the stock and mint, bring to the boil and simmer gently for about 5 minutes until the courgettes are just soft. Season to taste with salt and pepper.

5. Leave to cool slightly, then tip into the blender (in batches if necessary) and, starting on low speed, blend until smooth.

6. Return the soup to the pan, stir in lemon juice to taste, and reheat.

7. Serve each bowlful sprinkled with the crisp pancetta and garnished with mint leaves.

Beetroot Soup with Soured Cream and Dill

This simple adaptation of the Ukrainian soup called Borscht is made with ready-cooked beetroot (the type to be found in vacuum packs on the fresh salad counter). Serve it chilled in summer or hot at other times of the year.

Serves 6

Two 250g packets cooked beetroot
6 spring onions, chopped
400g can chopped tomatoes
1 tbsp clear honey
500ml/18 fl oz good-quality vegetable stock
2 tbsp lemon juice
Salt and freshly milled black pepper
1 tbsp finely chopped fresh dill
142ml carton soured cream

1. Put the beetroot (with its juice) into the blender with the onions, tomatoes and honey. Blend until smooth (you may need to scrape down the sides occasionally).

2. Tip into a large bowl (for chilled soup) or saucepan (for hot soup) and stir in the stock and the lemon juice. Season to taste with salt and pepper.

3. Either cover and chill until needed or heat gently until just bubbling.

4. Meanwhile, stir the dill into the soured cream.

5. Serve the soup in bowls, each topped with a spoonful of the dill cream.

Quick Gazpacho

Another soup that needs no cooking – just simple fresh and store-cupboard ingredients whizzed together in the blender. It's ideal for serving on hot days – at home, in the garden or on a picnic.

Serves 4-6

550g/1¼ lb ripe tomatoes, skinned, seeds removed, and chopped
1 small cucumber, skinned, seeds removed, and chopped
160g jar roasted peppers, drained and chopped
6 spring onions, sliced
2 plump garlic cloves, crushed
2 tbsp olive oil
2 tbsp red or white wine vinegar
115g/4 oz fresh white breadcrumbs (I like to use ciabatta)
2 tsp sugar
Salt and freshly milled black pepper
600ml/1 pt cold chicken stock, plus extra if necessary
Crisp croûtons, to serve

1. Put the tomatoes into a large bowl and add the cucumber, peppers, onions, garlic, oil, vinegar, breadcrumbs and sugar. Season with salt and pepper and stir well. Cover and leave to stand for 10-15 minutes, stirring once or twice.

2. Stir in the cold stock.

3. Tip into the blender (in batches) and blend until smooth.

4. If necessary, add extra stock until the consistency of the soup is perfect for serving, adjust seasoning to taste, then chill for 2 hours or more.

5. Serve with croûtons.

Chickpea and Pasta Soup

The anchovies give this soup a lovely rounded flavour, though you won't be able to taste them.

Serves 4

1 tbsp olive oil
1 medium onion, thinly sliced
1 garlic clove, sliced
1 red pepper, seeds removed, and sliced
2 anchovy fillets, chopped
200g can tomatoes
400g can chickpeas
300ml/½ pt chicken or vegetable stock
Salt and freshly milled black pepper
40g/1½ oz tiny pasta shapes

1. Heat the oil in a large pan and add the onion, garlic, pepper and anchovies. Cook gently, stirring occasionally, for 5-10 minutes until soft but not brown (alternatively put the ingredients into a casserole, cover and microwave on High for about 5 minutes, stirring twice).

2. Add the tomatoes and the chickpeas and their liquid.

3. Bring just to the boil, cover and simmer gently for about 10 minutes or until the pepper is quite soft (or cover and microwave on High for about 10 minutes).

4. Leave to cool slightly, then tip the mixture into the blender (in batches if necessary) and, starting on low speed, blend until smooth.

5. Return the soup to the pan (or microwave casserole) and add the stock, seasoning and pasta.

6. Bring just to the boil, then simmer gently for about 10 minutes (or microwave on High until the soup just boils, then cook on MEDIUM for about 10 minutes) or until the pasta is cooked.

7. Adjust the seasoning to taste and serve immediately.

Spiced Carrot and Coriander Soup

Particularly good served with hot naan bread or grilled pitta bread. Swirl a little cream on the top of each serving if you like.

Take care when handling the chilli – wash your hands thoroughly afterwards or, better still, wear thin rubber gloves to prepare it.

Serves 4

2 tbsp oil
1 small onion, chopped
1 garlic clove, crushed
1 tsp curry powder
1 tsp ground coriander
1 tsp ground turmeric
Salt and freshly milled black pepper
350g/12 oz carrots, sliced
1 small red chilli, seeds removed, and chopped
850ml/1½ pt vegetable stock
About 2 tbsp fresh coriander leaves

1. Heat the oil in a large pan, add the onion and garlic and cook for about 5 minutes, stirring occasionally, until soft but not brown (alternatively put the ingredients into a casserole, cover and cook on High for about 3 minutes, stirring once).

2. Add the spices and seasoning and cook for 1-2 minutes, stirring (or microwave on High for 1 minute).

3. Add the carrots, chilli and stock. Bring just to the boil, cover and simmer gently for about 20 minutes (or microwave on High until just boiling, then cook on MEDIUM for 15-20 minutes) until the carrots are very tender.

4. Leave to cool slightly, then tip the mixture into the blender (in batches if necessary) and, starting on low speed, blend until smooth. To the final batch, add the coriander and blend until chopped.

5. Return the soup to the pan (or microwave casserole) and reheat before serving.

Pea and Ham Soup

Probably the easiest soup you will ever make! Serve it with warm crusty bread. You could make the soup even more substantial by adding some shredded cooked ham just before serving.

Serves 2-3

25g/1 oz butter
1 medium onion, finely chopped
Two 300g cans processed peas
150ml/¼ pt ham stock, plus extra for thinning
2 tbsp dried skimmed milk
Salt and freshly milled black pepper

1. Melt the butter in a saucepan, add the onion and cook for about 8 minutes, stirring occasionally, until very soft but not brown (alternatively put the butter and onion into a casserole, cover and microwave on High for about 5 minutes, stirring once).

2. Add the peas (including their liquid) and stock. Bring just to the boil, cover and simmer gently for 5 minutes (or microwave on High until just boiling, then cook on MEDIUM for about 3 minutes, stirring once).

3. Leave to cool slightly, then tip into the blender and (starting on a low speed) blend until smooth.

4. Add the milk and blend briefly again. If the soup is too thick, thin it down a little by adding some extra stock.

5. Return the soup to the pan or casserole, season to taste with salt and pepper and reheat before serving.

Mediterranean Bean Soup

Follow the recipe for Mediterranean Beans on page 56, adding extra vegetable stock until you reach the right consistency.

8

SAVOURY TARTS AND OTHER DISHES

Tuna, Tomato and Caper Tart

For speed, I often use a ready-made plain pastry case bought from the supermarket.

Serves 4

142ml carton double cream
2 medium eggs
4 spring onions, chopped
185g can tuna, drained
2 tsp finely grated lemon rind
Salt and freshly milled black pepper
1 tbsp capers
20cm/8 inch cooked pastry case
1 large tomato, sliced
Lemon wedges, to serve

1. Put the cream, eggs and onions into the blender and blend briefly.

2. Add the tuna, lemon rind, seasoning and the capers and blend briefly.

3. Pour the mixture into the pastry case and arrange the tomato slices on top, pressing them gently just under the surface.

4. Cook in a preheated oven at 180°C/ 350°F/ Gas 4 for about 40 minutes or until set and golden brown.

5. Serve warm or at room temperature with lemon wedges for squeezing.

Tomato, Cheese and Herb Tart

Serve with a leafy salad, black olives and some Italian ciabatta bread.

Serves 4

200g can tomatoes
2 tbsp tomato purée
1 garlic clove, crushed
50g can anchovies, drained
Small handful of fresh herb leaves, such as oregano, basil, or chives
Freshly milled black pepper
20cm/8 inch cooked pastry case
2 tomatoes, sliced
115g/4 oz grated mozzarella cheese
2 tbsp freshly grated Parmesan cheese (optional)

1. Put the tomatoes into the blender followed by the tomato purée, garlic, anchovies, herbs and pepper. Blend on high speed until smooth, scraping down the sides if necessary.

2. Leave the pastry case in its container and stand on a baking sheet. Pour the tomato mixture into it, arrange the tomato slices on top and scatter the cheeses over.

3. Cook in a preheated oven at 200°C/400°F/Gas 6 for about 20 minutes or until golden brown and hot throughout.

4. Serve hot or warm.

Ham, Cherry Tomato and Thyme Tart

Skin the tomatoes if you wish but I leave them on and enjoy their flavour. Put the pastry into a metal flan dish – to encourage the base to cook.

Serves 4

6 thin slices of Italian dry cured ham, or an 80g packet
20cm/8 inch uncooked pastry case
12-16 cherry tomatoes
3 medium eggs
250g carton fromage frais
1-2 tbsp fresh thyme leaves
Salt and freshly milled black pepper
1-2 tbsp finely grated Parmesan cheese

1. Put a baking sheet in the oven while you preheat it to 200°C/400°F/Gas 6.

2. Arrange the ham slices over the base and sides of the pastry, overlapping them and allowing them to stand slightly higher than the pastry sides.

3. Scatter the tomatoes over the top.

4. Put the eggs into the blender, add the fromage frais, thyme and seasoning. Blend until smooth. Pour the mixture over the tomatoes.

5. Put the filled tart on the hot baking sheet in the oven and cook at 200°C/400°F/Gas 6 for about 35 minutes, sprinkling the cheese over the top for the final 10 minutes.

Cheese and Spinach Pie

Serve warm as a main course with crisp salad leaves or as a starter.

Serves 6-8

225g/8 oz spinach leaves, washed
2 large eggs
Two 250g tubs ricotta cheese
125g mozzarella cheese
25g/1 oz grated Parmesan cheese
Freshly grated nutmeg
Salt and freshly milled black pepper
6 sheets of filo pastry
Melted butter

1. On the hob (or in the microwave) cook the spinach, with just the water clinging to the leaves, for about 5 minutes or until wilted. Drain and press out excess liquid.

2. Put the eggs into the blender. Break the ricotta and mozzarella cheese on to the eggs. Add the Parmesan and spinach. Blend on medium speed until smooth. Season to taste with nutmeg, salt and pepper.

3. Brush a 23cm/9 inch square tin with butter and line with three sheets of pastry, brushing between each with butter and allowing the pastry to hang over the sides.

4. Pour the cheese and spinach mixture into the lined tin.

5. Top with the remaining pastry, brushing each layer with butter. Fold the edges over the top and brush with butter.

6. Bake in a preheated oven at 200°C/400°F/Gas 6 for about 30 minutes until the filling is set and the pastry is crisp and golden brown.

Chicken and Leek Pies

These well-filled pies are delicious hot, warm or cold, which makes them ideal for packed lunches and picnics.

Serves 4

About 400g/14 oz ready-rolled puff pastry
15g/½ oz butter
1 medium leek, thinly sliced
2 medium eggs
225g/8 oz chicken breast, cut into dice
Salt and freshly milled black pepper
1-2 tbsp fresh herb leaves, such as thyme, tarragon or parsley
Beaten egg, to glaze

1. Cut half the pastry into four circles, each large enough to line an individual pie dish (I usually use a four-hole Yorkshire pudding tin). Cut the remaining pastry into four lids.

2. Melt the butter in a small pan, add the leek and cook gently for about 5 minutes, stirring occasionally, until soft but not brown (alternatively, put the butter and leek into a small casserole, cover and microwave on High for about 3 minutes).

3. Put the eggs into the blender and add the chicken, seasoning, herbs and leek, scraping in any juices from the pan. Pulse on medium speed until well mixed and the chicken is finely chopped.

4. Spoon the mixture into the pastry cases, filling them generously. Brush the edges of the pastry with beaten egg and place the lids on top, pressing the edges together to seal them. Brush the tops of the pies with beaten egg and make a small slit in the centre of each.

5. Bake in a preheated oven at 200°C/400°F/Gas 6 for about 30 minutes until well risen, golden brown and cooked through.

Salmon Fries

Serve with a mixed salad or in split rolls with salad leaves, thin slices of red onion and lemon wedges for squeezing over.

Serves 2

250g/9 oz skinless salmon fillets, cut into 2.5cm/1 inch
 cubes
3 tbsp tartare sauce
2 tbsp chopped fresh dill or parsley
1 tsp finely grated lemon rind (optional)
1 spring onion, chopped
Salt and freshly milled black pepper
Olive oil for frying

1. Put the salmon into the blender with the tartare sauce, herb, lemon rind, onion and seasoning. Blend (pulse) on medium speed until fairly smooth.

2. Heat a little oil in a frying pan, add spoonfuls of the mixture and fry, turning once, until golden brown and cooked through. Serve immediately.

Feta and Olive Tart

A filling dish with Greek flavours. I like to serve it with a tomato salad. It's good served cold too.

Serves 4

2 large eggs
5 tbsp double cream
200g pack feta cheese, cut into cubes
2 tbsp chopped chives
About 8 green olives
20cm/8 inch cooked plain pastry case

1. Put the eggs into the blender and add the cream, cheese, chives and olives. Pulse on medium speed until well mixed and the cheese and olives are chopped.

2. Pour the mixture into the pastry case and bake in a preheated oven at 180°C/350°F/Gas 4 for about 30 minutes or until puffed and golden brown.

Falafel

Try this Middle Eastern snack – serve the Falafel in warmed and split pitta bread with shredded lettuce and thinly sliced tomato.

Serves 8-10 as a snack or appetiser

400g can chickpeas, drained
1 slice of bread
1 small onion, chopped
1 garlic clove, crushed
1 tsp ground coriander
1 tsp ground cumin
¼ tsp cayenne
Small handful of parsley sprigs
Salt and freshly milled black pepper
Oil for frying
Lemon wedges, to serve

1. Tip the chickpeas into the blender and blend on medium speed until puréed, scraping down the sides occasionally.

2. Break the bread into pieces and add to the blender with the onion, garlic, spices, parsley and seasoning. Blend on medium speed until finely chopped and well mixed, scraping down the sides occasionally.

3. Tip the mixture into a bowl, cover and chill for 1-2 hours.

4. With wetted hands, divide the mixture and shape into balls about 2.5cm/1 inch in diameter.

5. Heat the oil in a pan (the oil should be 2.5-5cm/1-2 inch deep) to about 180°C/350°F and fry the balls, a few at a time, for 2-3 minutes until crisp and golden brown.

6. Drain and serve with lemon wedges for squeezing over.

Prawn Sesame Sticks

A delicious Chinese-style snack that's ideal for serving with drinks. Use bread that is one or two days old.

Makes about 24

1 medium egg
1 tbsp rice wine or dry sherry
225g/8 oz peeled prawns
1 tbsp grated root ginger
2 spring onions, chopped
1 rounded tsp cornflour
Small pinch of ground star anise
Salt
4 bread slices
4 tbsp sesame seeds
Oil for frying

1. Put the egg and rice wine into the blender followed by the prawns, ginger, onions, cornflour, star anise and salt. Blend on medium speed to make a smooth paste, scraping down the sides occasionally.

2. Spread the paste thickly on one side of each bread slice and sprinkle the sesame seeds over.

3. Heat some oil in a deep frying pan and fry the bread, turning once, until crisp and golden brown on both sides. Drain on kitchen paper.

4. Cut each slice into six pieces and serve warm.

Fritter Batter with Beer

Ideal for dipping fish (try squid, prawns or strips of plaice) or vegetables (onion rings, pepper strips, aubergine slices) before deep frying.

Makes about 300ml/½ pt

175ml/6 fl oz beer
1 medium egg
1 medium egg white
15g/½ oz butter, melted
115g/4 oz plain flour
2-3 tbsp fresh herb leaves, such as parsley, thyme or coriander
Salt and freshly milled black pepper

1. Put the beer into the blender followed by the remaining ingredients in the order in which they are listed. Blend on high speed until smooth, scraping down the sides if necessary.

2. Cover and leave to stand until required, stirring well before using.

Pancakes

A must on Shrove Tuesday and delicious at any other time of the year!

Makes 8

300ml/½ pt milk
1 medium egg
15g/½ oz butter, melted
115g/4 oz plain flour
Pinch of salt
Oil for cooking
Sugar, to serve
Lemon wedges, to serve

1. Put the milk into the blender followed by the egg, melted butter, flour and salt. Blend on high speed until smooth, scraping down the sides if necessary.

2. Cover and leave to stand until required, stirring well before using.

3. Brush a little oil over the inside of an 18-20cm/7-8 inch heavy-base frying pan and heat until hot. Pour in just enough batter to thinly coat the base of the pan and cook for 1-2 minutes until golden brown.

4. Turn (or toss) the pancake over and cook the second side for about 1 minute until golden brown. Lift out and keep warm.

5. Repeat with the remaining batter to make eight pancakes.

6. Serve sprinkled with sugar and lemon juice squeezed over.

Yorkshire Puddings

Britain's traditional accompaniment to roast beef. For the best flavour, use the fat from the roast to cook the puddings. Do not be tempted to open the oven door until the puddings have risen and set (otherwise they will sink).

Makes 16 small

85ml/3 fl oz milk
1 large egg
Pinch of salt
115g/4 oz plain flour
Fat from the roast, beef dripping or oil

1. Put the milk in the blender with 85ml/3 fl oz cold water. Add the egg, salt and flour. Blend until smooth, scraping down the sides if necessary.

2. Cover and leave to stand until required, stirring well before use.

3. Preheat the oven to 220°C/425°F/Gas 7.

4. Put about ½ tsp fat into each of 16 patty or muffin tins and heat in the oven until very hot and beginning to haze.

5. Quickly pour the batter into the hot fat and return to the oven, cooking for about 15 minutes until well risen and golden brown.

9

SWEET TARTS AND OTHER DELIGHTFUL DESSERTS

Pear Frangipane Tart

If you like, glaze the cooked tart with a little melted apricot jam. Serve it warm or cold with a spoonful of thick cream or crème fraîche.

Serves 6

410g can pear quarters
85g/3 oz blanched or flaked almonds
2 medium eggs
2 drops almond extract
85g/3 oz soft butter
85g/3 oz caster sugar
1 tbsp flour
20cm/8 inch uncooked pastry case

1. Drain the pears, reserving 1 tbsp juice.

2. Put the almonds into the blender and pulse until finely ground. Tip on to a plate.

3. Put the eggs into the blender followed by the reserved pear juice, almond extract, almonds, butter, sugar and flour. Pulse on medium speed until smooth, scraping down the sides if necessary.

4. Spread the mixture over the base of the pastry case and arrange the pears on top, like the spokes of a wheel, pressing them into the batter.

5. Cook in a preheated oven at 170°C/325°F/Gas 3 for 30-35 minutes until set and golden brown.

Apricot and Almond Tart

Save yourself time and keep a ready-baked pastry case (bought from the supermarket) handy. Serve it warm or cold, with crème fraîche, whipped cream or custard.

Serves 6

20cm/8 inch cooked sweet pastry case
2 tbsp apricot jam
2 large eggs
1 tbsp milk
85g/3 oz ready-to-eat dried apricots
85g/3 oz soft butter
85g/3 oz ground almonds
55g/2 oz caster sugar

1. Put the pastry case on a baking sheet and spread the apricot jam evenly in the base.

2. Put the eggs and milk into the blender, followed by the apricots, butter, almonds and sugar. Blend on medium speed until the apricots are finely chopped and all the ingredients are well mixed (you may need to scrape down the sides occasionally).

3. Spoon the mixture evenly over the jam in the pastry case.

4. Cook in a preheated oven at 190°C/375°F/Gas 5 for about 30 minutes, until firm to the touch and deep golden brown.

Orange and Amaretti Custard Tart

A ready-made pastry case from the supermarket is ideal for this tart too. Serve it warm or chilled, with or without fresh fruit.

Serves 6

20cm/8 inch cooked sweet pastry case
142g carton double cream
2 large eggs
312g can mandarin orange pieces, drained
25g/1 oz amaretti biscuits or macaroons

1. Leave the pastry case in its foil container or tin and place on a baking sheet.

2. Put the remaining ingredients into the blender and blend on medium speed until well mixed.

3. Pour the mixture into the pastry case.

4. Cook in a preheated oven at 180°C/350°F/Gas 4 for about 40 minutes until set and golden brown.

Plum and Walnut Crunch Tart

Use ripe plums and serve it warm. It's also delicious with fresh ripe apricots and almonds or hazelnuts in place of plums and walnuts.

Serves 6

4 ripe plums, halved and stones removed
20cm/8 inch cooked pastry case
85g/3 oz walnuts
85g/3 oz demerara sugar
2 tbsp lemon juice
3 tbsp milk
200g carton cream cheese
55g/2 oz caster sugar
Finely grated rind of 1 lemon

1. Arrange the plum halves over the base of the pastry case.

2. Put the walnuts in the blender and pulse until roughly chopped. Tip out into a small bowl and mix with the demerara sugar.

3. Put the lemon juice and milk into the blender and add the cheese, caster sugar and lemon rind. Blend until smooth, scraping down the sides if necessary.

4. Pour the mixture over and around the plums and scatter the walnut mixture over the top.

5. Bake in a preheated oven at 200°C/400°F/Gas 6 for about 30 minutes (if the nuts start to get too brown, cover them with a small piece of foil).

Pear, Ginger and Marzipan Tart

If you have a very sweet tooth, you will love this. I like to leave the marzipan in small chunks but, if you prefer a smoother filling, whizz it in with the other ingredients in step 2. Serve the tart warm or chilled with Greek yogurt or crème fraîche.

Serves 6

115g/4 oz marzipan, cut into very small cubes
20cm/8 inch cooked pastry case
2 large eggs
410g can pears, drained
2 pieces stem ginger in syrup, quartered
1 tbsp ginger syrup

1. Scatter the marzipan over the base of the pastry case.

2. Put the eggs into the blender followed by the pears, ginger and syrup. Blend until smooth, scraping down the sides if necessary.

3. Pour the mixture evenly over the marzipan.

4. Bake in a preheated oven at 180°C/350°F/Gas 4 for 30-40 minutes until set and golden brown.

Curd Cheese, Lemon and Sultana Tart

Serve this tart warm or cold. If you like, decorate it with very thin strips of lemon rind and dust the top with icing sugar.

Serves 6

2 large eggs
Finely grated rind and juice of 1 lemon
1-2 tbsp brandy, rum or orange liqueur
250g/9 oz curd cheese
85g/3 oz caster sugar
20cm/8 inch cooked pastry case
55g/2 oz sultanas

1. Put the eggs into the blender, followed by the lemon rind and juice, brandy, cheese and sugar. Blend on medium speed until smooth, scraping down the sides occasionally.

2. Leave the pastry case in its foil container or tin and place on a baking sheet. Scatter the sultanas in the base and pour the cheese mixture over the top.

3. Bake in a preheated oven at 190°C/375°F/Gas 5 for about 40 minutes until set and golden brown.

Banana and Muscovado Tart

The creamy filling complements the crisp pastry. Serve it warm or cold and, if you like, with some freshly-sliced banana.

Serves 6

2 medium eggs
175g/6 oz fromage frais
1 tbsp lemon juice
1 tsp cornflour
55g/2 oz muscovado sugar
1 large or two small ripe bananas
20cm/8 inch cooked sweet pastry case

1. Put the eggs into the blender and add the fromage frais, lemon juice, cornflour and sugar. Break up the banana(s) and add to the blender. Blend on medium speed until smooth, scraping down the sides if necessary.

2. Pour the mixture into the pastry case.

3. Bake in a preheated oven at 180°C/350°F/Gas 4 for 30-35 minutes until firm to touch and golden brown.

Mocha Pots

These pots are very rich and creamy and so simple to make.
Serve them with crisp biscuits.

Serves 4

150g/5½ oz dark chocolate
1½ tbsp instant coffee granules
1 medium egg
2 tbsp caster sugar
1 tsp vanilla extract
Pinch of salt
150ml/¼ pt full cream milk
Cocoa powder or icing sugar for dusting

1. Break the chocolate into the blender and buzz briefly
    until chopped into small pieces.

2. Add the coffee, egg, sugar, vanilla and salt.

3. Bring the milk just to the boil, pour into the blender,
    cover and blend for about 1 minute until smooth.

4. Pour into small serving dishes (I like to use coffee cups)
    and chill for several hours.

5. Just before serving, sift a little cocoa or icing sugar over
    the top of each 'pot' (if you are using coffee cups, sit
    them on matching saucers and allow some of the
    powder to stray on to each saucer).

Walnut Cake

The recipe for this feathery-light cake has no added fat and is based on one served to me by an American friend. When the cakes are cool, sandwich them together with jam or marmalade and sprinkle the top with icing sugar.

Alternatively, make the Citrus Butter Cream Icing opposite and use half to sandwich and half to decorate the top.

Serves 6

3 level tbsp plain flour
2½ level tsp baking powder
3 large eggs
140g/5 oz caster sugar
100g/3½ oz broken walnuts

1. Preheat the oven to 180°C/350°F/Gas 4. Grease and line the base of two 20cm/8 inch sandwich cake tins with baking paper.

2. Sift the flour with the baking powder and set aside.

3. Break the eggs into the blender, add the sugar and blend for 1-2 minutes until the mixture is smooth and light.

4. Add the walnuts and blend until they are quite finely chopped.

5. Add the flour mixture and blend until just combined.

6. Pour the mixture equally into the tins.

7. Bake in the preheated oven for about 20 minutes until golden brown and softly firm.

8. Carefully run a knife around the edge of the cakes, turn out, remove the paper and leave to cool on a wire rack.

Vanilla Butter Cream Icing

Making butter icing is quick and foolproof in a blender, with none of those clouds of icing sugar that would normally envelop you.

Sufficient to sandwich and decorate the top of one 20cm/ 8 inch cake.

50g/2 oz soft butter
1 tsp vanilla extract
350g/12 oz icing sugar

1. Put the butter into the blender and add 3 tbsp hot water. Blend until smooth.

2. Add the vanilla and the icing sugar.

3. Cover and blend until smooth, scraping down the sides once or twice.

Almond Butter Cream Icing

Make the butter cream icing as above, replacing the vanilla extract with ½ tsp almond extract.

Chocolate Butter Cream Icing

Make the butter cream icing as above, adding 2 tbsp cocoa powder.

Citrus Butter Cream Icing

Make the butter cream icing as above, omitting the vanilla extract and adding the finely grated rind of 1 small orange, 1 lemon or 1 lime.

Coffee Butter Cream Icing

Make the butter cream icing as above, omitting the vanilla and adding 1-2 tbsp instant coffee or 2-3 tsp coffee essence.

Red Fruit Soup

Soup for dessert? Why not? This is so refreshing on a hot summer's day during the soft fruit season. Sometimes, I like to top each serving with a spoonful of thick Greek yogurt or whipped cream.

Serves 4

450g/1 lb mixed soft red fruit, such as raspberries, redcurrants and strawberries, plus extra for decorating
About 50g/1¾ oz icing sugar
1 tsp lemon juice
125ml/4 fl oz sparkling white wine
Sweet crisp biscuits, to serve
Fresh mint leaves, to decorate

1. Put the fruit, sugar and lemon juice into the blender.

2. Blend on medium speed, scraping down the sides once or twice if necessary, until smooth.

3. Pass the purée through a sieve to remove the seeds.

4. Stir in the wine and chill until required.

5. Serve in glass bowls or tumblers with crisp biscuits and decorated with extra fruit and mint leaves.

Chocolate Vanilla Creams

Serve these with crisp biscuits. Alternatively, top each serving with crumbled biscuits such as macaroons or amaretti.

Serves 4-6

175g plain chocolate, broken into squares
2 tbsp caster sugar
1 tsp vanilla extract
175ml/6 fl oz milk
85g/3 oz cream cheese

1. Put the chocolate in the blender and buzz briefly until chopped into small pieces.

2. Add the sugar and vanilla.

3. Heat the milk until hot but not boiling and add to the blender.

4. Blend on high speed, until the chocolate has melted.

5. Cut the cheese into cubes and add to the chocolate mixture and blend until smooth.

6. Pour into individual glasses or dishes and chill for at least 2 hours until set.

Summer Fruit Coulis

A fresh-tasting sauce that can be served chilled or warm with ice cream, yogurt, fresh or poached fruit, cheesecake, chocolate cake and so on. In winter months, I buy those packets of frozen summer fruit to make this.

Makes about 300ml/½ pt

250g/9 oz summer fruit, such as raspberries, strawberries, blackberries, blackcurrants
2 tsp lemon or lime juice
Icing sugar
2 tbsp fruit liqueur (choose a flavour to complement the fruit)

1.   Put the fruit into the blender with the juice and 2 tbsp sugar. Blend on high speed until smooth, scraping down the sides if necessary.

2.   Add sugar to taste, blending briefly after each addition.

3.   If wished, pass the sauce through a nylon sieve to remove the seeds.

4.   Stir in the liqueur and chill until required.

Chocolate and Coffee Sauce

Spoon this velvety sauce over ice cream, fruit (pears in particular) or chocolate pudding. Sometimes I add a table-spoon of rum or brandy.

Serves 4-6

1 heaped tsp instant coffee
115g/4 oz caster sugar
115g/4 oz plain chocolate, broken into squares

1.   Put the coffee into the blender and add 175ml/6 fl oz boiling water (from the kettle).

2.   Add the sugar and chocolate and blend until smooth.

Apricot and Orange Wedges

A favourite tea-time treat in our house. Sometimes I make it with ready-to-eat dried prunes in place of the apricots. Serve it warm or cold, just as it is or with cream, yogurt, ice cream or a fruit coulis (see opposite).

Serves 8-10

200g/7 oz plain flour
25g/1 oz semolina or polenta
75g/2¾ oz caster sugar
175g/6 oz chilled butter, cut into cubes
Finely grated rind and juice of 1 medium orange
250g/9 oz ready-to-eat dried apricots
Icing sugar, for sifting

1. Put the flour into the blender with the semolina, sugar and butter. Pulse on a medium-low speed until the mixture resembles breadcrumbs, stirring occasionally.

2. Spread half the crumb mixture in a 20cm/8 in flan or cake tin that has been base-lined with baking paper, pressing it down lightly. Reserve the remainder.

3. Put the orange juice into the blender, followed by the apricots and orange rind. Pulse on a medium-low speed until finely chopped, scraping down the sides occasionally.

4. Spoon the apricot mixture evenly over the crumb base.

5. Spread the remaining crumb mixture over the apricots and press down lightly.

6. Cook in a preheated oven at 180°C/350°F/Gas 4 for about 45 minutes until set and golden brown.

7. To serve warm, leave to cool for 10 minutes before cutting into wedges. To serve cold, leave to cool for 10 minutes before cutting into wedges then leave to cool completely before removing from the tin.

8. Before serving, sift a little icing sugar over the top.

Pineapple and Vanilla Baked Cheesecake

Rich yet light, this cheesecake is ideal for special occasions. The recipe was given to me by my friend, Pompa Barman, and I have adapted it only slightly.

Serves 10-12

175g/6 oz biscuits, such as digestive
55g/2 oz butter, melted
2 large eggs, separated
175g/6 oz caster sugar
2 tsp vanilla extract
Finely grated rind and juice of 1 lemon
2 level tbsp cornflour
400g/14 oz cream cheese
425g can pineapple chunks, drained

Topping:
284ml carton soured cream
40g/1½ oz caster sugar
1 tsp vanilla extract

1. Break the biscuits into the blender and pulse on medium-to-low speed until finely crushed. Stir the biscuit crumbs into the melted butter and mix well. Press the mixture firmly over the bottom of a 23cm/ 9 inch loose-bottom, spring-clip cake tin.

2. Put the egg yolks into the blender and add the sugar, vanilla extract, lemon rind and juice and cornflour. Blend on high speed until smooth, scraping down the sides if necessary.

3. Break up the cheese and add to the blender and blend until smooth.

4. Add the pineapple to the blender and pulse until roughly chopped. Tip into a large bowl.

5. In another bowl whisk the egg whites until stiff and fold into the pineapple mixture. Spread evenly over the biscuit base.

6. Cook in a preheated oven at 140°C/275°F/Gas 1 for about 1 hour 10 minutes or until set.

7. Meanwhile, make the topping by stirring together the three ingredients. When the cheesecake is just about set, pour the topping over the surface, carefully spreading it to the edges with the back of a spoon. Continue cooking at the same temperature for a further 10 minutes.

8. If it's convenient, leave the cheesecake to cool in the (switched off) oven – this helps to prevent it cracking.

9. When cold, chill for about 5 hours before removing from the tin and serving.

Streusal Topping

Sprinkle this over cakes or fruit-filled tarts before baking to give a lovely crunchy topping.

Sufficient to top a 20cm/8 inch cake or tart

3-4 tbsp plain flour
1 tsp ground mixed spice
50g/2 oz soft brown sugar
50g/2 oz nuts, such as walnuts or pecans
25g/1 oz chilled butter

1. Put the first four ingredients into the blender. Cut the butter into quarters and add.

2. Pulse on medium-low speed until the mixture resembles breadcrumbs.

Coconut and Mango Mousse

A delicately flavoured mousse, serve it with crisp sweet biscuits such as amaretti.

Serves 6

410g can mangoes
200ml carton coconut cream
25g/1 oz caster sugar
2 tbsp coconut liqueur
1 sachet powdered gelatine
142ml carton double cream
2 medium egg whites
Whipped cream, to decorate
Toasted coconut, to decorate

1. Tip the mangoes, with their juice, into the blender and add the coconut cream, sugar and liqueur. Blend on high speed until smooth.

2. Measure 4 tbsp boiling water (from the kettle) into a small bowl. Add the gelatine and stir well. Leave to stand for 1 minute, then stir well until dissolved (the liquid should be clear).

3. With the blender running, slowly add the dissolved gelatine to the mango mixture. Tip into a large bowl.

4. Whip the cream to soft peaks and fold in.

5. With clean beaters, whisk the egg whites until stiff and fold in gently and thoroughly.

6. Pour into six individual dishes or one large dish and chill until set.

7. To serve, decorate with whipped cream and toasted coconut.

Baked Marmalade Puddings

If you prefer, make one large pudding and cook for 30-40 minutes. Serve it with custard.

Serves 6

175ml/6 fl oz milk
2 medium eggs
1 tsp vanilla extract
115g/4 oz soft butter
225g/8 oz self-raising flour
½ tsp baking powder
140g/5 oz soft brown sugar
4 tbsp marmalade

1. Put the milk into the blender followed by the eggs, vanilla, butter, flour, baking powder and sugar. Blend until smooth, scraping down the sides if necessary.

2. Butter six individual foil or ovenproof dishes and, into each, spoon 2 tsp marmalade. Spread the batter over the marmalade.

3. Stand the dishes on a baking sheet and bake in a preheated oven at 180°C/350°F/Gas 4 for about 20 minutes until well risen and golden brown.

4. Leave to stand for a minute or two before turning out on to warmed serving plates or dishes.

Melon and Ginger Sorbet

A light dessert or starter. Serve it with some thin slices of really ripe melon such as Galia and decorate with mint leaves.

Serves 6

About 675g/1½ lb skinned, de-seeded and chopped ripe melon, such as Charentais
6 tbsp ginger syrup
115g/4 oz caster sugar
2 pieces stem ginger in syrup, drained and chopped

1. Put all the ingredients into the blender and blend until smooth.

2. Pour the mixture into a freezer container and freeze for about 2 hours until nearly solid.

3. Cut the semi-frozen mass into pieces, return to the blender and blend again until smooth.

4. Return the mixture to the freezer and freeze again for 2 hours or longer.

5. If necessary allow the sorbet to soften for a few minutes at room temperature before scooping out and serving.

Frangipane Pastry

A version of the delicious French Gâteau Pithiviers. Serve it warm or cold.

Serves 6-8

About 350g/12 oz puff pastry, thawed if frozen
115g/4 oz blanched almonds
3 medium eggs
1 tbsp brandy or rum
115g/4 oz soft butter
115g/4 oz caster sugar
25g/1 oz flour
Beaten egg, for glazing
Icing sugar, for dusting

1. On a lightly floured surface, roll out the pastry and cut into two circles, each measuring about 20-23cm/ 8-9 inches.

2. Put the almonds in the blender and blend on high speed until finely ground. Add the eggs, brandy, butter, sugar and flour. Blend on medium speed until smooth, scraping down the sides if necessary.

3. Place one pastry circle on a baking sheet and spread the almond mixture over it to within 2.5cm/1 inch of the edge. Brush the pastry edge with beaten egg and lay the second piece on top, pressing the edges gently to seal them. Scallop the edges and, with a sharp knife, lightly score a diamond pattern on the top.

4. Cover and chill for ½-1 hour.

5. Brush the top with beaten egg and cook in a preheated oven at 200°C/400°F/Gas 6 for about 30 minutes until puffed and deep golden brown.

6. Dust with a little sieved icing sugar and return it to the oven for a few minutes until glazed.

Plum Clafoutis

Here is a French dessert that is traditionally made with whole, unpitted black cherries. As well as plums, it works well with peaches and apricots. Serve the pudding warm, dusted with icing sugar and a jug of cream.

Serves 4-6

500g/18 oz plums, halved and stones removed
115g/4 oz caster sugar
300ml/½ pt milk
3 medium eggs
125g/4½ oz plain flour
Pinch of salt
Butter

1. Toss the plums with half the sugar and leave to stand for about 30 minutes.

2. Meanwhile, put the milk into the blender followed by the eggs, flour, salt and the remaining sugar. Blend on high speed until smooth, scraping down the sides if necessary.

3. Cover and leave to stand until required, stirring well before using.

4. Butter a shallow ovenproof dish, scatter the plums in it and pour the batter over.

5. Cook in a preheated oven at 180°C/350°F/Gas 4 for about 30 minutes or until the batter is cooked through.

Summer Fruit Fool

Use whatever combination of soft fruit is available. Sometimes, I replace half the cream with ready-made custard and
stir it in at the end of step 2. Serve in pretty glasses with crisp
sweet biscuits.

Serves 4

**450g/1 lb mixed soft fruit, such as raspberries,
    strawberries, blackberries, blackcurrants (thawed if
    frozen)**
Caster sugar
284ml carton double cream
**Fresh mint leaves and toasted flaked almonds, to
    decorate**

1.   Put the fruit into the blender and blend to make a
     smooth purée, scraping down the sides if necessary.

2.   Add sugar to taste, blending until smooth.

3.   In a large bowl, whip the cream to stiff peaks. With a
     large spoon, fold in the fruit purée.

4.   Spoon the mixture into glasses and chill until set.

5.   Decorate with mint leaves and almonds before serving.

Pecan and Maple Syrup Ice Cream

Here is a really quick ice cream that's sure to impress.

Serves 8-10

600ml/1 pt ready-made custard
6 tbsp maple syrup
115g/4 oz pecan nuts
600ml/1 pt whipping cream

1. Put the custard into the blender and add the syrup and nuts. Pulse until well mixed and the pecans are chopped.

2. In a large bowl, whip the cream to soft peaks. Add the custard mixture and gently fold in.

3. Pour into a freezer container and freeze for 2-4 hours until mushy.

4. Tip the mixture back into the cleaned blender and pulse to break up the ice crystals (the mixture should look quite smooth). Return to the freezer container and freeze until firm.

5. Allow the ice cream to soften slightly in the refrigerator before serving.

Banana Ice

Make this instant low-fat 'ice cream' with thinly sliced
bananas that have been popped into the freezer for an hour
or more. Add a splash of orange liqueur to the mixture too if
you like.

Serves 4

6 ripe bananas, peeled, thinly sliced and frozen
About 2 tbsp fromage frais
About 2 tbsp orange juice
1 tsp vanilla extract
Lemon juice

1. Allow the frozen bananas to stand at room temperature
   for 2-3 minutes.

2. Tip the bananas into the blender and blend on medium
   speed, scraping down the sides occasionally and adding sufficient fromage frais and orange juice to make a
   smooth, creamy consistency.

3. Add the vanilla and lemon juice to taste, blending until
   well mixed.

4. Serve immediately.

Crisp Granola

Great served for breakfast or as a snack at any time of the day.

Serves about 8-10

100g/3½ oz almonds, hazelnuts or brazils
250g/9 oz oats
75g/2¾ oz sunflower seeds
75g/2¾ oz pumpkin seeds
50g/1¾ oz sesame seeds
50g/1¾ oz coconut shavings
4 tbsp safflower or sunflower oil
4 tbsp honey
1 tsp vanilla extract
50g/1¾ oz raisins

1. Put the nuts into the blender and pulse on medium-low speed until roughly chopped.

2. Tip the chopped nuts into a large bowl and stir in the oats, seeds and coconut.

3. Put the oil, honey and vanilla into the blender and blend on medium speed until well mixed. Add the mixture to the bowl, stirring until the contents are well coated.

4. Spread the mixture in an even layer on a baking tray.

5. Bake in a preheated oven at 150°C/300°F/Gas 2 for about 45 minutes, stirring frequently, until golden brown and crisp.

6. Leave to cool (it will crisp up), stirring occasionally, then mix in the raisins.

Soured Cream Fruit Dip

This is a lovely way to finish a meal – sharing a dessert of fresh fruit and cream with friends. The recipe appears on page 45.

10

SHAKES, SMOOTHIES AND COCKTAILS

A Basic Milk Shake

Choose your flavour according to the ice cream.

Serves 2

300ml/½ pt cold milk
142ml carton double cream
4 scoops ice cream, such as vanilla
Few drops of vanilla extract

1.   Put all the ingredients into the blender and blend on high speed until smooth.

2.   Serve immediately.

Chocolate and Banana Milk Shake

Serve with chocolate finger biscuits or a flake to stir it!

Serves 2

300ml/½ pt cold milk
142ml carton double cream
4 scoops chocolate ice cream
1 tbsp drinking chocolate
1 banana, broken into pieces

1.   Put all the ingredients into the blender and blend on high speed until smooth.

2.   Serve immediately.

Mocha Milk Shake

Serve with a little drinking chocolate sprinkled over the top.

Serves 2

300ml/½ pt cold milk
4 tbsp double cream
4 scoops chocolate ice cream
1½ tbsp coffee essence

1. Put all the ingredients into the blender and blend on high speed until smooth.

2. Serve immediately.

Strawberry and Vanilla Milk Shake

Change the flavour with your choice of soft fruit – stoned cherries are a favourite of mine.

Serves 2

600ml/1 pt milk
115g/4 oz ripe strawberries
4 scoops vanilla ice cream
2 drops vanilla extract

1. Put all the ingredients into the blender and blend on high speed until smooth.

2. Serve immediately.

Banana and Mango Milk Shake

My daughters are grown up now, but they still like to top this shake with a scoop of coconut or vanilla ice cream.

Serves 3-4

1 large ripe banana
1 large ripe mango, stoned and peeled
150ml/¼ pt orange juice
150ml/¼ pt milk
1 tbsp clear honey
Orange slices, to decorate

1. Break the banana into the blender and add the mango, orange juice, milk and honey.

2. Blend on high speed until smooth.

3. Serve in chilled glasses, decorated with orange slices (hang them over the sides).

Strawberry Yogurt Shake

You couldn't get much simpler than this. Change the flavour with your choice of yogurt.

Serves 2-3

300ml/½ pt milk, chilled
500g (large) carton strawberry yogurt, chilled
2 ripe bananas
1 tbsp lemon juice

1. Put all the ingredients into the blender and blend until smooth.

2. Serve immediately.

Spiced Coffee Shake

I have served this topped with a swirl of whipped cream and sprinkled with some grated chocolate or sifted chocolate powder.

Serves 2

300ml/½ pt milk
300ml/½ pt black coffee
4 scoops vanilla ice cream
¼ tsp mixed spice

1. Put all the ingredients into the blender and blend on high speed until smooth.

2. Serve immediately.

Tropical Fruit Smoothie

Check that your blender is suitable for crushing ice. If not, simply omit the ice and you may like to serve the smoothie poured over an ice cube or two.

Serves 3-4

About 225g/8 oz ripe pineapple, peeled and cut into chunks
1 ripe mango, stone removed, and peeled
1 ripe banana
Squeeze of lime juice
About 4 ice cubes
Orange juice

1. Put the pineapple and mango into the blender, break in the banana and add the lime juice and ice cubes.

2. Blend on high speed, scraping down the sides if necessary, and adding enough orange juice to make a smooth, thick consistency.

3. Serve immediately.

Bilberry and Lime Smoothie

Bilberries or whinberries have a very short season. This is a delicious way to serve them and the lime juice complements their flavour beautifully. Blueberries can be used in their place.

Serves 3-4

225g/8 oz fresh bilberries
1 large ripe banana
3 tbsp clear honey
150g carton natural yogurt
Squeeze of lime juice

1. Put the bilberries into the blender and break in the banana. Add the honey and yogurt.

2. Blend on high speed, scraping down the sides if necessary, until smooth.

3. Blend in lime juice to taste.

4. Serve immediately.

Ice Cream Soda

A favourite of my husband, Huw. It can be made with soda water but he prefers it with a good-quality American cream soda.

Serves 2

600ml/1 pt American cream soda
4 scoops vanilla ice cream

1. Put the ingredients into the blender and blend on high speed until smooth.

2. Serve immediately.

Mango Lassi

Try serving this refreshing yogurt drink after a dish of curry.
Delicious! If your blender is suitable for crushing ice, add a
few cubes to the mixture in step 1.

Serves 3-4

3 ripe mangoes, stones removed, and peeled
150g carton natural yogurt
3 tbsp lime juice
2 tbsp clear honey

1. Put all the ingredients into the blender.

2. Blend on high speed until smooth.

3. Serve immediately.

Peach Cooler

I like to serve this in tall glasses with straws.

Serves 2-3

2 ripe peaches, stones removed, peeled and cut into
chunks
2 tbsp clear honey
600ml/1 pt milk, chilled
1 ripe banana

1. Put the peaches, honey and milk into the blender and
    break in the banana.

2. Blend on high speed until smooth.

3. Serve immediately.

Caribbean Cocktail

A non-alcoholic favourite of mine. Add ice cubes if you wish but first check that your blender is suitable for crushing ice.

Serves 2

1 banana
50ml/2 fl oz milk
50ml/2 fl oz lime juice
125ml/4 fl oz ginger ale

1. Break the banana into the blender, add the remaining ingredients and blend until smooth.

2. Serve in chilled glasses.

Citrus Special

Serve in large glasses, decorated with lemon, lime and orange slices.

Serves 2

Juice of 2 oranges
Juice of 1 lemon
Juice of 1 lime
125ml/4 fl oz grenadine (pomegranate-flavoured syrup)
2 tbsp double cream
Soda water

1. Put the citrus juices, grenadine and cream into the blender and blend until smooth.

2. Serve in chilled glasses and top up with soda water.

Fresh Fruit Cocktail

Check that your blender is suitable for crushing ice. If not, simply whizz up the fruit and pour it over ice cubes. Serve in chilled glasses, decorated with strawberries and mint leaves.

Serves 2

Juice of 1 orange
Juice of 1 lemon
8 large ripe strawberries
2 fresh pineapple slices
8 ice cubes

1. Put all the ingredients into the blender and blend on high speed until smooth.

2. Serve immediately.

Lemonade

A quick-to-make refreshing drink. Use unwaxed lemons and check that your blender is suitable for crushing ice.

Serves 3-4

2 lemons, scrubbed and roughly chopped
55g/2 oz caster sugar
10 ice cubes
Thin lemon slices, to serve

1. Put the ingredients in the blender and blend until well chopped. Add 600ml/1 pt cold water and blend again for 1-2 minutes.

2. Strain into a jug, float some lemon slices on top and serve.

Watermelon Lemonade

A very refreshing and pretty summer drink. For real impact, serve it in large tumblers decorated with large thin slices of watermelon and giant straws.

Makes about 1-1¼ litres/2 pints

1kg/2¼ lb watermelon, skin and seeds removed
125ml/4 fl oz fresh lemon juice
115g/4 oz sugar
Ice and lemon wedges, to serve

1. Chop the watermelon and put into the blender (in batches if necessary) with the lemon juice. Blend on high speed until smooth. Transfer to a large jug.
2. Put the sugar into a saucepan with 400ml/14 fl oz water and heat gently until the sugar has dissolved (alternatively, microwave on High, stirring frequently, until the sugar has just dissolved). Leave to cool.
3. Stir the sugar syrup into the watermelon and chill for at least 2 hours before serving.
4. Serve with ice and lemon wedges.

Bloody Mary

This cocktail looks good served in short tumbler glasses. Check that your blender is suitable for crushing ice.

Serves 2

100ml/3½ fl oz vodka
200ml/7 fl oz tomato juice
Dash of Worcestershire sauce
Dash of Tabasco sauce
Squeeze of lemon juice
About 15 ice cubes

1. Put all the ingredients into the blender.
2. Pulse on high speed for about 15 seconds each time until slushy, scraping down the sides of the blender if necessary.
3. Serve immediately.

Margarita

Serve this in chilled glasses that have had their rims dipped in lime juice and then coarse salt. Check that your blender is suitable for crushing ice.

Serves 2

200ml/7 fl oz tequila
100ml/3½ fl oz triple sec liqueur, orange curaçao,
   Cointreau or Grand Marnier
50ml/2 fl oz freshly squeezed lime juice
About 15 ice cubes
Lime wedges, to decorate

1. Put all the ingredients, except the lime wedges, into the blender.

2. Pulse on high speed for about 15 seconds each time until slushy, scraping down the sides of the blender if necessary.

3. Serve immediately decorated with lime wedges.

Piña Colada

Serve in chilled tumblers with straws and decorated with fresh pineapple slices and cherries. Check that your blender is suitable for crushing ice.

Serves 2-3

200ml/7 fl oz pineapple juice
150ml/¼ pt white or golden rum
100ml/3½ fl oz coconut cream
About 10 ice cubes

1. Put all the ingredients into the blender.

2. Pulse on high speed for about 15 seconds each time until slushy, scraping down the sides of the blender if necessary.

3. Serve immediately.

Frozen Daiquiri

To serve, pour into chilled glasses that have had their rims dipped in lime juice and caster sugar. Check that your blender is suitable for crushing ice.

Serves 2-3

200ml/7 fl oz white rum
Juice of 1 lime
1 tbsp caster sugar
About 15 ice cubes

1. Put all the ingredients into the blender.

2. Pulse on high speed for about 15 seconds each time until slushy, scraping down the sides of the blender if necessary.

3. Serve immediately.

Banana Daiquiri

Follow the recipe for Daiquiri, adding 2 large ripe bananas, broken into pieces.

Peach Daiquiri

Follow the recipe for Daiquiri, adding 4 ripe, peeled and stoned, peaches.

Strawberry Daiquiri

Follow the recipe for Daiquiri, adding 450g/1 lb fresh ripe strawberries.

INDEX